Releasing the Ability of God Through Prayer

by

Charles Capps

Unless otherwise indicated, all Scripture quotations are taken from the *King James Version* of the Bible.

Over 300,000 in Print

20 19 18   12 11 10

Releasing the Ability of God Through Prayer
ISBN-13: 978-0-9820320-2-2
Formerly ISBN-10: 1-57794-669-3
Formerly ISBN-13: 978-1-57794-669-4

Published by Capps Publishing
Copyright ©1978 by Charles Capps
PO. Box 69
England, Arkansas 72046

Contents

Introduction

It is not my intention in this book to do a comprehensive study on prayer. In no way is this book to be considered the last word on prayer. I will be the first to tell you if your prayer life is successful, I wouldn't change it. If not, I would admonish you to change.

This book is not meant to be controversial; however, it will probably be contrary to everything religious you have ever heard about prayer. Yet it is my responsibility to share it with you. You can do what you want to with it. If it is too strong for you, put it on a shelf; but don't forget where you put it because you will need it someday.

So many people have prayed to a God who was hard to entreat and slow to hear, one who had to be pestered day after day, until one day maybe He would be persuaded to answer their prayer. When the truth came, they found there was no such God in the Bible. For God says, *Ask and it shall be given you . . . everyone that asketh receiveth.*

The Lord spoke to me several years ago, saying, "Forget your preconceived ideas and study My Word as though you had never heard it before." When I began to do that, I learned some things, and then I had to unlearn some other things. So much of my religious thinking was contrary to the Word of God.

Someone has aptly stated, "If you have been on the same road for twenty years and haven't arrived at your destination, you should know you are on the wrong road."

I traveled the road of religious praying for more than twenty years and seldom ever saw any results. I was confused, disillusioned, sick in body, and supernaturally in debt. I was hanging on to the last knot at the end of my rope. I had prayed, pleaded, begged, and complained, but the answers had not come. I had a zeal for God, but not according to knowledge. I was on the wrong road. When I found the truth (the Word of God), the knowledge of that truth set me free.

The reason for this book is found in 2 Timothy 2:24-26: *And the servant of the Lord must not strive; but be gentle unto all men, apt to teach, patient, in meekness instructing those that oppose themselves; if God peradventure will give them repentance to the acknowledging of the truth; and that they may recover themselves out of the snare of the devil, who are taken captive by him at his will.*

I recovered myself out of the snare of the devil by acting on God's Word, and you can do the same. Read this book prayerfully; it is dedicated to your freedom.

1

The Ability of God

Every born-again believer has God's ability abiding in him in the person of Jesus Christ; yet few have ever learned to release that power. God is in you to the degree that His Word is in you. God and His Word are one. *In the beginning was the Word, and the Word was with God, and the Word was God* (John 1:1). The Word was God in the beginning. The Word is still God today. God's Word is Lord over every circumstance of life. Our minds cannot grasp these truths without the revelation that God and His Word are one.

Jesus said, *If ye abide in me, and my words abide in you, ye shall ask what ye will, and it shall be done unto you* (John 15:7). We stagger at the love and faith which God has invested in humanity. *If a man love me, he will keep my words: and my Father will love him, and we will come unto him, and make our abode* (our home) *with him* (John 14:23).

The spirit must be expanded by the rebirth to receive such awesome truths as Jesus spoke when He prayed to the Father: . . . *the glory which thou gavest me I have given them; that they may be one, even as* **WE ARE ONE:** *I in them, and thou in me, that they may be made perfect in one that the world may know that thou* . . . **hast loved them, as thou hast loved me** . . . *And I have declared unto them thy name, and will declare it: that* **the love wherewith thou hast loved me may be in them, and I in them** (John 17:22-26).

Hebrews 1:3 literally says Jesus was the exact expression of God's substance. He was the exact personality of God. "I and my Father are one." Truth personified. *The Word was God . . . upholding all things by the word of his power.* God released His ability in Word form, and it upholds all things. The whole universe stands in obedience to His Words. **God's ability is in His Word.** We must learn to release that ability within us by rightly dividing His Words.

Jesus said, *These things I have spoken unto you, that in me ye might have peace* (John 16:33). Many of God's people are held in bondage because the enemy has perverted their minds to the great truths of the Word of God. God gave you His Word to put you over. He designed it to work in every area of life. His Word works and it knows no time or distance. It is spiritual law.

God's Word Rules

God's Word is alive and powerful. (Heb. 4:12.) It is living substance. It is law in the world of the Spirit. It is more powerful than the laws of nature that govern the universe today.

The law of gravity works continually. You won't wake up some morning on the ceiling, wondering why the law of gravity isn't working!

No, you can rest assured that when you wake up in the morning, you will be lying down; you won't be lying up on the ceiling.

Just that sure are God's spiritual laws and they work continually. They work the same yesterday, today, and forever. They will never change. The Word says, *God changeth not.*

God's Word never changes, but it changes things.

Laws of God

Let us take off our religious eyeglasses and look at some things that Jesus said concerning prayer. There are laws of God that govern and uphold all things. I want you to see that the laws we will be referring to are God's laws and they are spiritual. God is a Spirit and *He* created the universe. Everything you see has been created by a Spirit.

Now sometimes people get the idea that this is the real world and the spirit world just somehow doesn't exist because they can't see it with the natural eye. It is like a fog out there somewhere. Many people believe in it like they do Santa Claus. The spirit world is the real world. This is not the real world. The Word says, *the things which are seen are temporal* (2 Cor. 4:18). In other words, they are subject to change.

But *the word of God . . . liveth and abideth forever* (1 Peter 1:23). God's Word is a living Person (Jesus) and abides forever. The reason you have eternal life is because you received the eternal Word into your spirit and He is life. The Word is eternal and He produces after His kind.

Scriptural Bondage

Today there are many Christians who have been deceived by the evil one. Satan is called the deceiver. His ability is in his deception. Jesus stripped him of his authority and power. God's Word will always strip the armor from satan and bring to light his deception.

Deception is his only armor. God's Word will penetrate that armor and expose him.

Many are held in bondage by certain scriptures. Have you noticed that the devil tried to put Jesus in bondage by quoting scriptures? Now the enemy knows a few scriptures, but he will quote them out of context to bring you into bondage.

If you take scripture out of context, you can make the Bible say anything you want it to say. For example, the Bible says that Judas went out and hanged himself. Then in another place Jesus said, "Go thou and do likewise." If you take these two scriptures out of context and put them together, you could say that the Bible says it is all right to go hang yourself. Well, some folk have. They have hanged themselves spiritually by doing so.

Certain scriptures hold people in bondage because they *seem* to say things which they do not say at all. If you learn to rightly divide the Word, it will produce liberty. It will also produce power and strength in your life. Just as food will produce physical strength for the body, so will the Word of

God produce spiritual strength for the spirit man. We need to feast on the Word and be doers of it.

It Is Written

On the mount of temptation (Luke 4) Jesus spoke three words that shook the foundation of satan's kingdom beyond repair: **It is written.** Jesus stood on a sure foundation and refused to speak anything except what His Father said.

Notice, when all else failed to move Jesus off the Word, satan himself began to quote scripture. The last and greatest of all deceptions is to take the Word out of context and distort it to make it say something different from the true meaning.

This was his double-barrel shot, his last ditch stand: *Cast thyself down from hence: For it is written, He shall give his angels charge over thee, to keep thee: And in their hands they shall bear thee up, lest at any time thou dash thy foot against a stone.*

You will notice the enemy quoted it almost word for word from Psalm 91:11-12. He drew it out of context to infer that Jesus could not commit suicide even by jumping off the pinnacle of the temple. Psalm 91:9-13 is a beautiful passage of scripture promising protection from evil, plagues, and accidental destruction; but in no way does it apply to a willful act of self-destruction.

In this, you see what I believe is satan's ultimate deception to Christians today. He distorts men's minds with religious thinking that causes the very opposite meaning to be magnified and covers the true meaning with the garbage of intellectual reasoning.

He has done this with the great truths that Jesus taught concerning prayer. He has a reason: **Effective prayer will destroy his kingdom of darkness and release the ability of God in the earth.**

As the Church of Jesus Christ comes to the knowledge of its authority in prayer as a joint-heir with Christ, it *will* partake of His divine nature. Then shall the Church proclaim boldly, **It is written!**

2

Prayer Is a Key

Prayer is a key to heaven's storehouse, but faith unlocks the door.

A prayer without faith is like a key without a hand to turn it.

In 1 John 5:14-15 we find some great truths about prayer: *And this is the confidence that we have in him, that, if we ask any thing according to his will, he heareth us: And if we know that he hear us, whatsoever we ask, we know that we have the petitions that we desired of him.*

Let's read it again and look at some key words. "This is the *confidence*." Or, this is the *faith*. We *have* this confidence in Him, that if we ask *any thing,* according to His will, He hears us. "And if we *know* that He hears us, *whatsoever* we ask, we *know* that we *have* the *petitions* that we *desired* of Him."

Notice that two key words here are *anything* and *whatsoever.* John said you can ask *anything* that you desire and have *whatsoever* you ask. If we know that He hears us, we know that we have what-soever we desired of Him.

If God hears you, if you get an audience with Him, you already have granted to you as your present possession what you ask.

Asking According

Now somebody says, "Yes, but that's if it is the will of God for you to have it." Well, let's look at verse 14 again: <u>*This is the confidence that we have in him, that, if we ask any thing*</u>. . . . Now why would he say *any thing,* if it has to be His will before it will work?

Let's say it this way so you can see it, "If you ask according to His will for asking." His Word is His will. This passage is not dealing with God's will for you to have or not to have a certain thing. This is not even involved in this verse of scripture. Many have thought it was and it has held them in bondage for years. *77*

They said, "If I pray for something that is not God's will, then I won't receive it."

Therefore, they didn't take time to find the will of God, but prayed saying, "Lord, if it be Your will." There was no faith in that prayer.

No need of praying that prayer. You are wasting your time. You do not know whether God has heard you, so you cannot release faith in your prayer. That prayer will not produce for you because it does not qualify on the basis of God's rules for asking. Answered prayer is governed by spiritual law (God's Word).

Many times our prayers have gone unanswered because we did not determine the will of God before asking. Therefore, we could not release faith *?*

Determine the will of God

in that prayer. Then on other occasions we have prayed beyond God's ability to answer. If He did do what we ask, He would violate His Word.

God's will concerning your having or not having is not involved in verse 14. Now don't misunderstand me. I am not saying you should pray for just anything whether it is God's will or not, but you can do that. The Bible says you can. If you know He heard you, *you will have* whatever you desired, you will have the petitions you requested—right, wrong, good, bad, or indifferent.

It is very dangerous for a person to pray for something assuming that it is God's will. *You can believe and receive things that are not God's will.* Israel received a king to rule over them. It wasn't God's will, but they requested it.

Be Specific

Now there are some things that are immaterial with God. Whether you drive a blue car or a red car doesn't matter to Him unless it matters to you.

According to the Word in Mark 11:24, if you desire
a red one, pray for a red one. Don't pray for just a
car—be specific!

God has set a spiritual law before us. If we will
learn to operate under the rules of His law, we will
get our prayers answered.

If we know that he hears us, **whatsoever we
ask**. . . . The idea present in verse 14 is to ask
according to God's will for asking.

I want to show you why you cannot interpret
that verse the way most people have, namely, "if it
is God's will for you to have it." The Bible says in
the mouth of two or three witnesses let every word
be established; so let's go to the Word of God and
find some more witnesses. Let's learn to interpret
the Word of God in the light of the rest of the
Bible. Don't just take one verse of scripture and
say, "That is what He said and that is all there is to
it." That can hold you in bondage. For instance,
here it seems to be saying something that it really
doesn't say.

If you ask *any thing* according to His will He hears you. He is talking about your asking according to God's rulebook for asking, His will for asking. What is God's will for asking?

. . . let him ask in faith, nothing wavering. For he that wavereth is like a wave of the sea driven with the wind and tossed. For let not that man think that he shall receive any thing of the Lord. A double-minded man is unstable in all his ways (James 1:6-8).

That is one of the rules for asking anything from God.

Whatsoever

Now for another witness let's go to Mark 11, verses 23 and 24. Here Jesus is teaching the greatest faith principle the world has ever known. It will absolutely transform your life.

Whosoever shall say unto this mountain, Be thou removed, and be thou cast into the sea and shall not doubt in his heart, but shall believe that those things which he saith shall come to pass; he shall have whatsoever he saith. He didn't say he would have what he believed God for. He didn't say he would have what he hoped for. He said he would have *whatsoever he saith.*

Then He connects that verse of scripture to the next one by saying it will also work in prayer. *Verse 23* is *not* a prayer scripture. It is the faith principle. It is spiritual law. Just as the law of gravity will work, so will this law work when it is applied correctly.

Verse 24 is the prayer scripture. *Therefore* it will work in prayer. *Therefore I say unto you, What things so ever ye DESIRE. . .*. Notice the words *ye desire.* It doesn't say what God desires, does it? No. Now let's put it in our language. He said, "Whatever you desire when you pray, you believe that you receive, and you shall have it."

Someone has said, "Oh, but if it's not God's will, you can't have it. So go ahead and pray for it; and if it's God's will, you will receive. If it isn't, you won't receive it anyway.

17

I beg your pardon! The Bible says you will. People are deceived in this area. Israel wanted a king. It wasn't God's will for them to have one, but they received a king. That is why it is so very important that *you learn God's will before you pray.* It would be better for you to spend a week reading and searching the Word of God before you ever form your prayer, than to just pray and assume it is God's will.

In Ecclesiastes 5:1-2 we find this admonition: When you go into the house of the Lord, let your words be few. Then in Psalm 37:7 we read, *Rest in the Lord, and wait patiently for him.* The Hebrew translation says, "to be silent to the Lord." Sometimes we do too much praying or we pray the wrong way at the wrong time.

For instance, a man, as he was being robbed, cried out, "Oh God, don't let them find that $100 bill I hid in my shoe." Now that's dumb! He told the thief what he needed to know. Sometimes we give satan valuable information while praying. We should learn when to be silent and when to pray. Prayer will get you into more trouble than you know how to handle, if it is not in line with the Word of God, or if it is not done accurately. The effectiveness of prayer is governed by spiritual law.

Sometimes people say that prayer couldn't hurt anyone. That is like saying, "Electricity cooks my food and washes my clothes and no one could get hurt by electricity." Well, as long as you use it wisely and obey the laws that govern that power, it will work for you. But the same force that washes your clothes and cooks your food can also destroy you if you violate the laws that govern that force.

7/7/2016 LR

Rules That Govern

Prayer is designed to work for you, not against you. The Word of God was designed to work for you; but when you cross up the rules, it is like trying to play baseball with football rules. It does not work. Sometimes we use the wrong rules in prayer.

There are different kinds of prayer and there are different rules for each kind. There is the prayer of dedication, the prayer of thanksgiving and praise, the prayer of intercession, and the prayer of petition.

In this book we are talking about the prayer of petition. Don't get the rules for the prayer of dedication and worship mixed up with the prayer of petition. When you do, you get the thing shorted out and it won't work. Rightly divide the Word of Truth; search out these rules and apply them correctly. Then your prayers will move heaven and earth in your behalf.

In fact, we read in the Word of God in Philippians 2:9-10, John 16:23, and Mark 16:17-18 that Jesus has been highly exalted and has been given a name above every name, and He has given that name to us to control the force of evil. The authority of this earth has been given to man. We have authority to petition God by prayer and move the forces of heaven in our behalf. We have authority in prayer by the words of our mouths to bind evil forces—the powers of darkness—and render them harmless and ineffective against us. We do not need more power; we just need to apply the spiritual laws that God has given us.

Jesus said, *What things soever ye desire, when ye pray, believe that ye receive them, and ye shall have them* (Mark 11:24). Didn't say a thing about God's will, did He? This is one verse of scripture that would contradict the interpretation of 1 John 5:14, "if it is God's will. "

God's Word Abiding in Us

Now let's go to another witness. Jesus said, *If ye abide in me, and my words abide in you, ask what* **God will?** NO! *Ask what* **ye will,** *and it shall be done unto you* (John 15:7). It doesn't say a thing about God's will. Ask what *you* will. But if the Word of God abides in you, then you are going to frame your prayer accurately according to the Word of God and you are not going to pray for things that you know are not the will of God.

It would be foolish if you had a financial need to pray that someone would lose their billfold so you could find it and get their money. That would be evil.

The Bible says in James 4:2-3, *Ye have not, because ye ask not. Ye ask and receive not because ye ask amiss.* Here James is not talking about asking for something that *just* wasn't God's will. He goes further and deeper than that. The word *amiss* means evil. Ask evil.

If you read on, you will find out what the problem was. He says to them, "ye adulterers and adulteresses." They were probably praying for someone else's wife, and that was evil!

If you pray for things you know are evil, your heart will condemn you and your faith will not work.

Wouldn't it have been wonderful if Jesus had said, "If ye abide in me, ask what ye will and it shall be done." Oh, praise God, that would have been great! Everyone who is born again could just ask what they want, and there it would be. But it doesn't work that way. Jesus said, *If ye abide in me,* **and my words abide in you,** *ask what ye will and it shall be done.*

Sometimes people pray, "Dear Lord, I cast this care on You and I believe You to take this care, and

I praise You, Father, that the need is met." But before they get out of church, they say, "You know I am so worried. I just don't know what I am going to do." The Word did not abide in them.

If ye abide in me and my words abide in you, ask what ye will and it shall be done unto you. Someone says, "Oh, if I ask what I will, that would be selfish." Read the next verse: *Herein is my Father glorified that ye bear much fruit.* Do you believe that it is God's will for the Father to be glorified? Every time you get your prayer answered, it glorifies the Father.

Now do you see how you can build wrong thinking by using one verse of scripture alone? I remember something I read in one of Kenneth Hagin's books several years ago. He made a statement that I will never forget: "People that think wrong believe wrong; when they believe wrong, they act wrong." That is one of the main problems in the church world today. Many people believe wrong because they think wrong. They are right in their hearts but wrong in their heads.

Know God's Will

Sometimes we pray for things we don't need and are not good for us. I heard of a man in World War II who prayed for God to move him from one concentration camp to another just a few miles away. He prayed and God answered his prayer. He was very happy, but it was short lived. In a few weeks the Allied forces came into the camp he left and liberated all the prisoners. He stayed two more years in the other camp. He used his faith and his prayer was answered, but it prolonged the problem.

First of all, you need to **determine what is the will of God.** When you know God's will, you know that God is going to hear you. The Word says if God hears you, you will get what you ask. First John 5:14-15 is simply saying that if you get an audience with your Father, you will get your prayer answered.

When I was growing up, I knew if I could get to my dad, I could get that nickel I wanted to take to school the next day. But sometimes my mother would say, "No, don't bother him now. He is asleep." So I couldn't get an audience with him. I knew if I could get an audience with him, I would get what I wanted. The Word tells us how to get an audience with our Heavenly Father.

Sometimes we think the Lord must have heard us because we have goose bumps running up and down our back. That has nothing to do with it. You may get some feeling (and that's all right), but don't base your faith on feelings. What if you don't get any feeling at all? That's all right, too. That doesn't change the Word of God.

. . . let him ask in faith, nothing wavering. For he that wavereth is like a wave of the sea driven with the wind and tossed. For let not that man think that he shall receive any thing of the Lord. A double-minded man is unstable in all his ways (James 1:6-8).

You receive because you believe God and act on His Word. Goose bumps will never produce an answer to prayer—*faith will!*

3

New Covenant Prayer

In the day that Jesus was teaching, they were operating under the Law. The prayer that Jesus taught His disciples to pray was under the old covenant. You will notice that it did not include the name of Jesus. New Testament prayer is prayed in the name of Jesus.

The new covenant prayer is different, for it is governed by the rules of the new covenant. The New Testament is a new contract. It is the will of the Lord Jesus Christ, sealed with Jesus' own blood. It is established on better promises. If the old had been perfect, it would not have passed away; but finding fault with it, God made a new covenant (see Heb. 8:6-8). And this is your new contract.

There are many people who have been saved and filled with the Spirit for years, yet have never read their contract. They are quick to tell you that you never know what God will do. They don't realize that their new contract reveals what He will do!

And in that day ye shall ask me nothing. Verily, verily, I say unto you, Whatsoever ye shall ask the Father in my name, he will give it you (John 16:23). Here Jesus is beginning to teach the disciples new covenant rules for prayer.

In that day. What day is He talking about? After the day of Pentecost, when the Holy Ghost has come—in that day when the new covenant is in operation—then, *ye shall ask me nothing.*

You see, Jesus supplied every need the disciples had while He was with them. He also fed the multitude in the wilderness. When Peter needed some tax money, Jesus told him to go fishing and the first fish he caught would have the tax money in its mouth. Jesus healed the sick, raised the dead, and cast out demons.

Even with all this taking place, He turned to them one day and said, *It is expedient for you* (or it is better for you) *that I go away, for if I go not away, the Comforter will not come unto you* (John 16:7). In other words, "Until I go away, the Holy Ghost will not come and the new covenant will not be in force." Jesus said that this new covenant was even better for us than if He had stayed here on earth. *He that believeth on me, the works that I do shall he do also; and greater works than these shall he do; because I go unto my Father* (John 14:12). We were to do the greater works after the Holy Ghost came.

The Will of our Covenant

And in that day ye shall ask me nothing. Verily, verily, I say unto you, Whatsoever ye shall ask the Father in my name, he will give it you. Hitherto have ye asked nothing in my name: ask, and ye shall receive, that your joy may be full (John 16:23,24). If your joy is not full, then you need to ask so that you may have *the full joy* Jesus promised. His will for us under the new covenant is that *our joy be full.*

Jesus taught us to pray to the Father in the name of Jesus. We have authority to use His name, but we are not to pray to Jesus.

Somebody says, "Yes, but the Lord knows what I mean." Well, that is true. I am sure the Lord does know what you mean, but He doesn't answer prayer just because He knows what you mean; He answers prayer when you pray according to His rulebook—the Bible. You must fulfill your part of the covenant or contract.

Faith Makes Prayer Work

The one element that makes prayer work is faith. Faith is a spiritual law designed to unlock the treasures of the unseen. Sometimes people will classify this one or that one as a faith teacher. If you teach the Word of God, you are a faith teacher. The Word of God is the Word of faith. (Rom. 10:8,9.)

Prayer gets its power from faith, and faith works by love. Somehow down through the years we have gotten the idea that prayer makes faith work. It doesn't. Faith makes prayer work. **Faith will work without prayer, but prayer will not work without faith.** You can put your faith to work through prayer. *And the* **prayer of faith** *shall save the sick, and the Lord shall raise him up* (James 5:15).

Prayer Does Not Change God

But when ye pray, use not vain repetitions, as the heathen do: for they think that they shall be heard for their much speaking (Matt. 6:7).

Jesus cut away some religious theology right there.

I had always heard that if you just kept praying, God would finally answer you. "Just keep on praying, keep bombarding the gates of heaven!" Some think if you can get more people praying, you will finally talk God into it.

But you are not going to change God by your praying. God said, *I am the Lord, I change not* (Mal. 3:6). You can change yourself by praying and getting yourself in line with the Word so God can answer. **Prayer changes things, but it does not change God.**

Hezekiah is a good example of this. God sent a prophet to tell him to get his house in order for he was going to die. Hezekiah turned his face to the wall, prayed, repented, and changed his position before God.

Then God said, "You will live fifteen more years."

Many think that he prayed and changed God's mind. For years I thought that was true, but he didn't change God's mind. It was God's will all along that he live a full life, but Hezekiah got out of His will and God said that this would cause him to die a premature death. When he repented, God said, "Now you will live."

You do not change God by your praying, for He does not change. For years I thought God didn't want me to have whatever I was praying about, so

I was trying to talk Him into letting me have it. I thought my job was to keep pestering Him like I did my earthly daddy, until He changed His mind just to get rid of me. No, God does not operate that way. Faith moves God, not prayer alone.

Vain Repetitions

But when ye pray, use not vain repetitions, as the heathen do (Matt. 6:7). Remember that we are talking about *the prayer of petition.* Someone says, "What about Jesus? He prayed the same prayer three times in the Garden." That was *the prayer of dedication*—"Not My will, Lord, but Thine be done."

You can pray the prayer of dedication over and over, but when it comes to a petition, be specific and rest in the Word of God.

Remember the 400 prophets of Baal. Elijah said, "You offer your sacrifice and the god that answers by fire, he will be God." So they cried, begged, and pleaded, and Elijah said, "Why don't you cry a little louder; maybe he is asleep." They began to cry louder and even cut themselves.

These are the heathen that Jesus was talking about when He said, *Use not vain repetitions as the heathen do*. They just kept praying the same thing. They prayed from morning on into the evening to no avail.

Then Elijah had twelve barrels of water poured on his sacrifice and prayed a short prayer just once and down came the fire.

It is not the length of the prayer that moves God. Nor will you be heard for your "much speaking." God answers prayer on the legal ground of the new covenant. We have authority to use the name of Jesus. We have a covenant with the Father through Jesus. Jesus has sealed it with His blood, and God will honor the name of Jesus. That name is above every name.

Don't Pray the Problem

I remember being in a service one night in a certain church, and a lady stood up and said, "I want you all to pray for my husband; he is getting worse. He won't go to church, and I have been praying for him every day for 25 years. He just keeps getting meaner."

The Spirit of God spoke up on the inside of me and said, "She has been holding fast to the problem all these years. If she had prayed in faith, she wouldn't have prayed all those other 24 years. She would have praised Me and thanked Me that My power was working in his behalf, and her husband would have been saved many years ago. But she has bound Me from the situation by the words of her mouth."

Now there is no doubt in my mind that every time she prayed for her husband, she said, "My husband is getting meaner. He is not getting any better. He won't go to church with me." And the Word teaches that you shall have what you say.

(Mark 11:23.) Now you can see the mistake she made.

Jesus said, *Whatsoever things ye desire, when ye pray, believe that ye receive them.* She didn't desire for her husband to get meaner. She didn't desire for him to stay at home. Why was she praying that way? She was deceived by satan and held in bondage by the words of her own mouth. In fact, she was holding her husband in bondage also. She had taken him out of God's hands and He couldn't work on her behalf, because in prayer she was saying the things she did not desire. She was holding fast to the problem.

Pray the Answer

Never pray your problem. If you pray the problem, it will get worse. If you pray the problem, you loose the ability of the enemy. Pray the problem, and it will grow greater and your faith will flee away on the wings of doubt.

Pray the thing you desire.

Go to the Word of God and find out what God said about it. You will find that the Word says, *What things soever ye desire, when ye pray, believe that ye receive them* (Mark 11:24).

So you would pray the desire: "Father, I desire my husband to be saved and filled with the Holy Spirit. I ask You to send laborers across his path to witness to him. As I am praying right now, I believe that I receive it in the name of Jesus. I cast all my cares over onto You; and when I get up in the morning, I will not pray about it again. I will continue to thank You, for it is done."

Now you have returned God's Word to Him, and He said that it will not return to Him void. When you return God's Word to Him, He will perform it.

Now that may not happen overnight. This is where the force of patience is exercised. Learn to be silent to the Lord as is mentioned in Psalm 37:7. Don't use vain repetitions. Don't pray the same prayer over and over. That will hold you in bondage.

I am a farmer by trade, and let's say that I have just planted a field of cotton. Now wouldn't it be foolish if I went out the next morning and said, "Man, something is wrong. This cotton is not coming up. Let's plow it up and plant it again." Then the next day the same thing happened.

If I kept doing that, I could plant 365 days and still not produce any cotton. We need to become as smart in the spiritual realm as we are in the natural. That kind of farming practice will cause you to go bankrupt quick!

Our prayers many times have held us in bondage, causing spiritual bankruptcy. No one would dare plant a garden and the next morning dig it up. It takes time for these things to happen.

God has certain laws that He operates under. He has regulated Himself by His Word. God has the power to do anything. But so many times He can't use His power in our behalf because if He did, it would violate His Word. That is one thing God cannot do! He cannot violate His Word. If He did some of the things we ask, He would have to lie to do it. We have prayed beyond His ability to answer because of our violation of His rules concerning prayer.

Jesus said, *What things soever ye desire, when ye pray, believe that ye receive them.* Some of you have been praying all the bad things, the problems. If God did what you really desired, then He would violate His Word. He said that you can have what you say when you pray, and you have said the problem in prayer over and over until all you are seeing and believing is the problem.

Have you ever prayed, "Lord, it is not working out. It is not getting any better"? Well, I was praying that very prayer one morning and the Lord spoke something into my spirit. It wouldn't have been any louder if I had heard it in my ears.

He said, "What are you doing?"

I said, "Lord, I am praying."

He said, "No, you are not; you are complaining!"

A lot of folks are complaining, thinking they are praying. They are telling God their problems. In

Matthew, chapter 6, Jesus said that the Father already knows the problem.

He already knows what you have need of before you ask Him. Then there is no need to pray the problem. What we need to do is zero in on the answer. *Pray and speak the answer; cast the problem over on Him.*

Satan's Deception

Satan has deceived Christians into praying the problem. Did you know the more you *pray* the problem, the more you *say* the problem? The more you *say* the problem, the more you will *believe* in the problem. The problem will grow because you are keeping it always before you.

It is just like fertilizing the problem. It will grow bigger. You tell others about it and they will say, "Yeah, you sure do have a problem." They will agree with you, and then they will tell someone else. Finally, you will have fifty people agreeing that you have a problem. *Then you **do** have a* *problem!* For Jesus said, *If two of you shall agree on earth as touching any thing . . . it shall be done* (Matt. 18:19).

Now you can see the deception of satan. He has deceived us by twisting the Word of God around so we use it against ourselves. Satan doesn't care how often you pray. He doesn't care how much you go to church. If he can distort the Word of God so that your prayers are ineffective, he has defeated you. Yes, you may make it to heaven, but you may not do anything while you are here on earth, except suffer, struggle along, and feel sorry for yourself.

Many people get the idea that they are just suffering for Jesus; when, in fact, if they would just act on the Word of God and stand against the enemy, rebuking him in the name of Jesus, they could live in victory. There is victory in the name of Jesus. *Submit yourselves therefore to God. Resist the devil, and he will flee from you* (James 4:7).

4

Accurate Prayer

Prayer Is a Legal Right

Under this new covenant contract, sealed by the Lord Jesus Christ in His own blood, you have the legal right as a born-again believer to enter the throne room of God. You can stand in His presence without fear, without a sense of inferiority, without a sense of guilt, because of what Jesus did. It is your legal right to come boldly before the throne of grace to request heavenly intervention in this earth on your behalf.

Prayer is your legal right, but you should come by the rules of spiritual law that govern prayer. Even though you don't, the law will still work—the law that says, *he shall have whatsoever he saith.* Or the law that says, *What things soever ye desire, when ye pray, believe that ye receive them, and ye shall have them.* These laws still work regardless of our ignorance of the Word.

Prayer is the legal right to ask God to supernaturally intervene in your behalf.

The power of binding and loosing is not in heaven. It is on the earth. *You* are the one who has authority to bind the forces of evil. *You* are the one who has the power to loose the ability of God in this earth through the prayer of faith.

It is your legal right to use the prayer of faith to put you over in life.

Wrong words in prayer will hold you in bondage. They will loose the ability of the enemy against you. Right words in prayer will release the ability of God.

44

Prayer is to line ourselves up with the Word of God and set ourselves in a position to give God liberty to move on our behalf.

Sometimes our prayers have bound God. If you rightly divide the Word of God in prayer, you will loose God's ability. It will cause you to stand in a new realm of faith. You will come to the point that you won't have to pray all night. You can pray, knowing that God hears you. Then you will be silent to the Lord. (Ps. 37:7.)

Faith Comes From the Word, Not Prayer

I once heard someone say, "I prayed all night about a certain situation, just stayed up and prayed all night." Well, if they had prayed in faith, they would have gone to sleep. Pray in faith, then rest in the Lord. When you start praying in faith, your words will be few, but they will be effective.

Sometimes we pray just trying to muster up some faith. That is not scriptural. Faith comes by hearing the Word of God, not by praying. (Rom. 10:17.) Go to the Word of God and hear the Word until faith comes; don't be too quick to pray. Sometimes we start talking before we know what to say. Hear the Word . . . hear the Word . . . hear the Word. It might take a week or a month, but *faith will come.*

Then go to God with the prayer of faith and thank Him. You won't have to stay there long. You can get more from God in two minutes, believing Him, than you can praying all night in unbelief.

Speak Faith-Filled Words in Prayer

There are several ways that you can release the ability of God within you. You can release God's ability in prayer. You can release God's ability through speaking faith-filled words. If you will team both of these together, *speaking faith-filled words in prayer,* then it will become a mighty force working for you. We are dealing primarily with releasing the ability of God through prayer, through *accurate* prayer. **Inaccurate prayer, if answered, will spell trouble.**

What Prayer Is Not

Before going any further, let's find out what prayer is *not*.

Prayer is *not* telling God your problem. Jesus said, *Your Father knoweth what things ye have need of, before ye ask him* (Matt. 6:8). For years, I thought to pray was to tell God the problem. No, that is not prayer.

Telling God the problem is complaining.

Prayer is not trying to change God's mind. God changeth not.

Have you ever wondered why Jesus said, *Whatsoever ye shall bind on earth shall be bound in heaven: and whatsoever ye shall loose on earth shall be loosed in heaven* (Matt. 18:18). All heaven will stand behind what you say in prayer. But not only will it work in prayer, it will also work in the things you speak. You can loose the ability of satan against yourself by the words of your mouth, even in prayer.

In Matthew, chapter 6, Jesus is teaching His disciples principles of prayer, and Jesus knew how to teach prayer accurately. If anyone knew how to pray, I believe Jesus did. So let's see what Jesus said about prayer:

But when ye pray, use not vain repetitions as the heathen do: for they think that they shall be heard for their much speaking. Be not ye therefore like unto them; for your Father knoweth what things ye have need of, before ye ask him (Matt. 6:7,8).

Notice Jesus said that the Father knows the need *before* we ask Him. So we can determine from the Word of God that you don't get your prayer answered because you need it answered. I believe we can safely pull that out of this scripture and say it is a fact from the Word of God: Praying is *NOT* telling God your need.

Some people have prayed, "Lord, I need this," and "Lord, I need that." He knows, but He doesn't answer prayer on the basis of need. If He did, there would be no needs.

Need is not what moves God; faith does.

Vain repetitions do not move God; faith does.

Much speaking does not move God; faith does.

Praying the same prayer over and over does not cause God to move; faith does. Asking according to His will for asking **will** move God. **When you pray, believe you receive; that moves God.**

We have often prayed, "Father, if it is Your will, let it be done." If it is not, we will just go on suffering, thinking we are being humble, when we are really being ignorant of God's Word. We need to know *who* determines whether or not our prayer is answered.

God is not the one who determines the outcome. *You* determine whether or not you receive. It would be good if we could just cast all that on the Lord and say, "Oh well, if it's God's will, it will work out, and if it isn't, it won't." That is a cop-out. I did it for years until I realized that it wasn't working.

If your prayer life is working, if you are getting your prayers answered, I wouldn't change the way I was praying. But if not, I would change it. I tried it the other way and it didn't work for me. I changed it and found something that works. If you have been on the same road for twenty years and haven't yet arrived, you should know that you are on the wrong road. Let's get on the right road by being accurate in prayer.

God's Word Is His Will

A prayer accurately formed and stated from the Word of God will absolutely move heaven, earth, and the things under the earth in your behalf.

We put faith in men to the point that we will work for a man a week, two weeks, or a month just because he said, "I'll pay you so much at the end of the week or month." We never doubt his word. We never check into his finances or have him checked out to see if he is capable of paying. We just believe he will because he said he would.

But when it comes to God's Word, sometimes we say, "Well, I don't know. You never know what God will do." But when you *know* what God will do, He will do it. (1 John 5:15.)

I realize some have prayed ten years about the same thing and have never seen it manifested. While I was praying one morning, the Spirit of God spoke to me, saying, "Don't ever pray for anything you can't believe. It will destroy your faith." Many have overloaded their faith.

Go to the Word of God and find out what the Word says about your situation. Whatever it is—if it is physical matters, finances, healing for the body—go to the Word of God and study to find out what God says about it. Determine God's will concerning the matter from His Word. Then when you find it, accurately form your prayer from the Word of God. Then petition the Father with it according to His Word, in faith, believing that you receive *when you pray.*

5

Keys to Answered Prayer

One of the keys to answered prayer is **to believe you receive when you pray.** *What things soever ye desire, when ye pray, believe that ye receive them, and ye shall have them* (Mark 11:24).

The faith principle of Mark 11:23 states that you can have what you say. It is a faith principle which you can employ every day by speaking right words. Another key to answered prayer is **to speak in agreement with your prayers daily.** Control the words that come out of your mouth.

For example, one day I was having a problem with a tractor. It had given me trouble a couple of times and I wanted to say, "That thing comes apart every time I take it to the field." I knew better than to say it, but it just rose up within me and it wanted to come out so bad. I told my wife I would just love to make a bad confession here, but I didn't dare do it. I have trained myself to believe that what I say will come to pass. My mind is renewed to God's Word.

Jesus went on to say in verse 24 that it will also work in prayer. You can use the same principle in prayer. *He* **shall have** *whatsoever he saith.* He didn't have it then, but he shall have it. Many Christians cancel their prayer with unwise words.

Believe and Receive

Mark 11:23 is a faith principle. It is not a prayer scripture. Verse 24 says, *Therefore* (or because of this faith principle) *I say unto you, What things soever ye desire when ye pray, believe that ye receive them and ye shall have them.*

Whatsoever **things**—whatsoever *things* ***you*** ***desire.*** He didn't say, "If it is God's will for you to have it." He said *Whatsoever things you desire when you pray, believe that you receive them.*

Now when are you going to believe that you receive them? You are not going to believe it when you see it, if you go by the Word of God. You must believe it *when you pray.* He said, "When you pray, *believe.*" What is the evidence that I received when I prayed? *Faith is the evidence of things not seen* (Heb. 11:1).

If I believed that I received this morning when I prayed, I wouldn't dare get up tomorrow morning and pray the same prayer. That would be proof that I hadn't believed.

Somebody says, "But it has not manifested yet." It doesn't say, "Believe when it is manifested." *When ye pray, believe that ye receive them, and ye shall have them.* It doesn't say you *have* them, but you *shall have* them. They are not manifest yet, but you have received God's Word. Therefore you have received them in your spirit.

How can you receive something that is not manifest yet? You receive it in your spirit. Your spirit man receives it as done. When you are praying, you are operating in spiritual law. You are operating in the spirit realm, not in the intellect. You are tapping the spiritual resources of God. You need to realize, in doing this, that you don't have the same physical evidence that you do when you are operating in the natural realm.

Things may look worse after you have prayed. In fact, some have told me, "You know, after we agreed in prayer, it got worse." Don't get excited about that. Did you believe when you prayed? Did you believe when we agreed you received it? The thing that will determine whether you believed it or not is this: When the circumstances look worse, do you still believe what we agreed upon?

For instance, you are needing a certain amount of money and you pray believing you receive. When you get up the next morning, you find the car won't start and the washing machine breaks down. Are you still believing that your financial needs are met? Most people won't. They will say, "Oh, dear Lord, just as I figured, it didn't work out."

Religious Praying

There is such a thing as prayer just to be praying. We might even call it religious praying. It is praying just because it seems like the thing to do—not believing anything, just praying. Evidently, this was the case in Acts 12. James had been killed and Herod proceeded to take Peter also.

Peter therefore was kept in prison: but prayer was made without ceasing of the church unto God for him (v. 5).

You find that the whole church was praying; but it must have been religious praying for, when the angel let Peter out, he went to the house of John Mark's mother where *many* were praying:

And as Peter knocked at the door of the gate, a damsel came to hearken, named Rhoda. And when she knew Peter's voice, she opened not the gate for gladness, but ran in, and told how Peter stood before the gate (vv. 13,14).

Up until now, everything seems to be rather normal, but listen to the confession of those who were praying: *And they said unto her, Thou art mad. But she constantly affirmed that it was even so. Then said they, It is his angel. But Peter continued knocking: and when they had opened the door and saw him, they were astonished* (vv. 15,16).

Rhoda's Faith

Evidently, Rhoda was the only one who agreed with what they were praying. Their saying surely was not in line with their praying, was it? *Thou art mad . . . It is his angel.* To them, Peter was already dead! I wouldn't want people praying for me like that! The servant girl, Rhoda, was the only one in the whole house who believed the answer when it appeared, and everyone thought she had gone crazy. I am glad the Bible doesn't hide these things because it lets *us know* that they were human. They would only believe Rhoda's faith confession after they saw Peter.

I really believe that Rhoda was the only one in that whole prayer group who had prayed in faith. Evidently, she had already prayed and was cleaning the house while everyone else was too busy being religious to open the door for Peter. The way they talked, I suspect that they were praying the problem. If it hadn't been for someone praying and believing the answer, they would have prayed Peter right into his grave.

Prayer alone does not bring deliverance. **It is the prayer of faith that brings deliverance.**

Conceived in Your Spirit

Here is the simplest way I know to put it: When you believe God and release your faith in prayer, it is conceived in the womb of the spirit and will be manifested. It will be brought forth, if you hold fast to your confession of faith.

It is as though a child is conceived in his mother's womb. When you believe you receive, your answer is then conceived in your spirit. Time may pass before it is manifest; but just as sure as a child will be delivered from his mother's womb, so will the answer to your prayer come forth in due season.

You have need of patience that after you have done the will of God, you will receive the promise of the Father. (Heb. 10:36.) Patience is a spiritual force which undergirds your faith and causes you to be constant through the trial.

Here is one of the problems. So many times we have thought God said to hold fast to the prayer. But that is not it at all. He told us not to use vain repetitions as the heathen who think God will hear them because of repeating it over and over. No. That is not what God said in His Word. He said, *When ye pray, believe.*

So I am going to release my faith when I pray. Therefore if I release my faith when I pray, He says that I *shall have it.* It is settled then. It is finished, thank God. I don't care if it looks worse in the morning, I will not take it up again in prayer, but will hold fast to my confession.

Now let me qualify some of those statements. If you go for a long period of time and your request is not manifested but is still getting worse, you have missed it somewhere. If you have missed it, admit it and ask God where you missed it. You have missed it somewhere if it is not working.

The Law of Sowing and Reaping

If you have a note due in January for $10,000, don't wait until December 29th to ask God to meet that need or to confess that your need is met according to His riches in glory. You have waited too late. That would take a miracle and we are not talking about miracles at this point. You need to start by putting the seed in the ground and proclaiming that your need is met. The law of sowing and reaping is a law of God, and it works.

Here is what has happened in many cases. People have started saying, "Oh, Lord, it looks worse. There is a recession on and I won't have the money by the end of the year. I'll never be able to meet the payment. We will never be able to do it." They confessed that for six months. Then when the note came due, they didn't have the money, but they were very pleased that they were able to prophesy it six months ahead of time.

The law of sowing and reaping was set in motion and produced failure. They spoke unbelief in prayer and they got what they said. Then they wondered why it worked out that way.

The very principle that God gave us to put us over, we have used in reverse. It will work just as fast in reverse gear as it will in forward.

I have heard people say, "I prayed, but I believe it is getting worse." "I prayed, but I'm afraid it is not working out." Well, I am not afraid. I know it is not working out because you are not releasing faith in God. You are releasing faith in the devil.

Fear is the reverse gear of faith. Fear brings satan on the scene. Fear releases the ability of satan against you. Faith releases the ability of God on your behalf. So when you pray, believe right then that it is settled. **Believe when you pray, and the manifestation will come.**

This is not a fairytale. The Word of God is true and it works. It is spiritual law. The Word is your contract with God the Father. You need to read your contract and know what is in it.

Unforgiveness and Prayer

Many times we stop at verse 24 in Mark 11, but let's go on to verses 25 and 26. Have you ever noticed that every time Jesus taught on prayer He mentioned forgiveness? If my prayers were not being answered, the first question I would ask myself would be, "Am I holding something against someone?" or "Have I forgiven those who have done me wrong?"

Jesus said, *And when ye stand praying, forgive, if ye have ought against any: that your Father also which is in heaven may forgive you your trespasses.*

But if ye do not forgive, neither will your Father which is in heaven forgive your trespasses.

I was meditating on this verse one day and decided that this may be the reason so many people kneel to pray. Jesus said, *When ye* **stand** *praying, forgive.* Maybe they think if they kneel, they don't have to forgive!

If I was having trouble with my prayer life, I would check to be sure I was walking in forgiveness. Unforgiveness will stop your faith from working. **Unforgiveness is a thief of life and a thief of faith.**

God's Will for the Earth

Knowing God's will is a key to answered prayer. So often people spend a lot of time trying to figure out if it is God's will for them to be healed or if it is God's will for them to be prosperous. Jesus said, *After this manner therefore pray ye: Our Father which art in heaven, Hallowed by thy name.*

Thy kingdom come. Thy will be done in earth, as it is in heaven (Matt. 6:9,10).

Let's ask ourselves what it is like in heaven:

Is there any poverty in heaven? No.

Is there any disease in heaven? No.

Jesus told His disciples to pray that the will of God be done in earth as it is in heaven. Then He must be saying to pray that there be no disease on this earth and that there be no poverty here. Now if Jesus is teaching His disciples to pray this way, don't you know that is the will of God? His will is that it be on this earth *as it is in heaven.*

When satan is put in the bottomless pit and shut up for a thousand years, there will be no sickness or disease. Now that ought to tell us where it comes from.

Sometimes people get the idea that God is testing and perfecting us with sickness and disease. They say that the trial of your faith perfects it. But that is not what the Word says. James says that the trying of your faith works patience. (James 1:3.)

How many of us have *not* had any trials and tests in life? If it were true that God uses trials and tests to perfect our faith, then every one of us would be perfect.

The trials of life are a design of satan to destroy you, not to perfect you.

The trying of your faith works patience. Patience is a spiritual force that comes into play to undergird your faith and to hold it up like a pier under a long span of a bridge. If the bridge didn't have piers to support it, it would collapse. That is what happens to many people's faith. It collapses for lack of patience. The trying of your faith causes the force of patience to come into place and undergird your faith. It causes you to be consistent through the trial and test that the enemy brings against you.

So often we have thought it was God sending us the trials and tests. No, thank God, it is not my Father sending them—it is satan. Jesus said, *The thief cometh not, but for to steal, and to kill, and to destroy: I am come that they might have life, and that they might have it more abundantly* (John 10:10).

Is there going to be any sickness and disease in heaven? No. Is there going to be any poverty there? No. There is abundance in that place. It is a healthy place. Do you know any poverty-stricken folk on earth who have their driveway paved with gold? The streets of that city are not only paved with gold, they are pure gold. The whole street is gold!

God's will is that this earth be conformed to the spirit world that spawned it. This universe is a creation of God and it was designed to be prosperous. But satan entered into it and fouled it up by distorting God's creation and His Word.

The Source of Trials and Temptations

And lead us not into temptation, but deliver us from evil (Matt. 6:13). Most people believe that the Lord sends the trials, tests, and temptations of life. I wonder why Jesus said to *pray that you enter not*

67

into temptation if the trials and temptations come from God?

If God knows everything and we know the Word says God has all knowledge, then I wonder why God would have to try and test us to find out what we would do in a certain situation. The Word also says that Jesus is the author and finisher of our faith. (Heb. 12:2.) Now since Jesus has authored our faith, God does not need to try it. He knows it will work. *Satan is the one trying our faith.*

Jesus said, *Lead us not into temptation, but deliver us from evil.* What evil is He talking about? The evil of trials and temptations. We can rise to a new level of faith when we realize that it is the thief that steals, kills, and destroys. It is Jesus who gives life abundantly. When you draw the battle line, you will have 50% of the battle won. This will set you at liberty in your prayer life.

You can use your faith shield to quench every fiery dart of the devil. But until you determine the cause, you cannot use your faith. You can't believe the thing will go away if God put it on you. It may not be time for it to go away. The enemy suggests that God might be using this to perfect you. It sounds logical, but it is a stronghold of the devil.

Now let me refresh your memory in this area. In Luke 8:22, Jesus said to the disciples, *Let us go over unto the other side,* then He fell asleep in the back of the ship.

A storm of wind arose on the lake and waves were lapping into the boat. The disciples began to say, *Master, we perish.* Jesus arose and *rebuked* the wind and the sea. Then He asked them, "Where is your faith?"

Was that storm sent of God to try their faith? No. That storm was designed by satan to get the Word out of them and it worked very well. (Mark 4:15.) They told Jesus what the devil said. The devil had told them that they would all drown. But Jesus said, "We are going to the other side." His Words did not abide in them.

In I John 3:8, we find that Jesus came to destroy the works of the devil. If the storm was of God, then Jesus destroyed the work of His Father. No,

Jesus came to undo everything that satan was doing. Jesus rebuked the wind because the storm had been caused by satan. He has perverted nature and used the atmosphere to bring floods, storms, and tornadoes. But headlines proclaim, *God Visited Our City Last Night With a Tornado.* No greater lie has ever been told!

When lightning struck a certain plant in Arkansas, it blew up, killing several people and injuring many others. The newspapers called it *an act of God.* No bigger lie has ever been told. Those things are perversions of nature. Satan has perverted the things God created for good. Genesis 1:31 says, *And God saw everything that he had made, and behold, it was very good.*

Lightning was what killed Job's cattle. The *King James Version* calls it "fire from heaven." One translation says "lightning." In other words, satan used the elements of the earth and atmosphere to destroy Job's cattle. But Job said, *The Lord giveth and the Lord taketh away,* which is actually recorded in the Bible. But Job was not under the anointing when he said it. He was deceived. He thought it was God, but you can plainly read in Job, chapter 1, that it was the devil who had caused Job's problems.

If you believe that God brings these things on you, you cannot use your faith to get rid of them.

There is no place in the Bible where it says, "Take the shield of faith and quench all the fiery darts of God"! You wouldn't dare pray for deliverance from something God is using to perfect you.

But when you get the battle line drawn and see that the thief comes to steal, kill, and destroy and that Jesus came to give us abundant life, then you can use your faith. You will be able to pray accurately. You can come against the evil forces and prevail. *Above all, taking the shield of faith, wherewith ye shall be able to quench* **all** *the fiery darts of the wicked* (Eph. 6:16).

When we have financial problems, most of the time it is the devil's work. Sometimes it is our own fault. It is *not* God, trying to teach us something! When we have problems in areas of the physical body, it is an attack of the enemy, because Jesus said for us to pray, *Thy will be done in earth as it is in heaven.*

God's will is that we walk in health on this earth and that is the way we should pray. *Beloved, I wish above all things that thou mayest prosper and be in health, even as thy soul prospereth* (3 John 2).

Act in Agreement with God's Word

You know we have sung that song, "When we all get to heaven, we'll sing and shout the victory." We have put victory off until then; but if we would learn to act on the Word, we could shout the victory here on earth. Jesus said we are to pray, *Thy will be done in earth, as it is in heaven.* It is God's will that we have victory here and that we shout it here on earth. But this doesn't come overnight.

I am a pilot, but I didn't learn to fly an airplane in one day. It took me months of study and practice. The first few lessons I thought I would never learn, but each time it became easier. The first time I saw one of those big 747s, I didn't believe it would fly.

I thought the thing was too big and too heavy. It will fly, but just because it will fly does not mean that I can fly it. I would have to learn.

You could say, "Well, I believe in prayer, then prayer ought to work for me," in the same way you could say, "I believe in flying; therefore I ought to be able to fly." Just because you believe in flying does not mean you can get in that 747 and fly it. You might get it off the ground, and you might get in trouble, to say the least!

Well, what makes us think the Word of God is any different? If we are going to operate in the Word accurately, we will have to spend time learning.

It is the same with the law of electricity. If you don't understand the laws that govern electricity, you are liable to get into trouble. The same power that will wash your clothes and cook your food and heat your house will kill you if you violate the laws that govern it. The Word of God is no less powerful. It operates on laws that will work when applied by *whosoever will*.

If I got in an airplane and said, "Well, I know that the book says if you are going to climb over a 50-foot obstacle in 1200 feet, you must use 20-degree flaps, but I just don't feel like it. It looks to me like it ought to clear the hanger without flaps." It doesn't matter how I feel or how it looks, I better go by what the book says or I am going to be in trouble.

So are our prayers in trouble when we don't use God's rulebook. When you do things accurately according to the Word of God, you have all heaven behind you and the Word will work for you.

God's Word Is the Answer

We could sum it up by saying that prayer is not telling God the problem. *Whatever you desire* is what you should pray, not the problem. Turn loose of the problem. Take hold of the answer and make it your prayer and your confession of faith.

As an example, let's say you have a financial need. You would pray, *Father, in the name of Jesus,*

Your Word says that You will supply all my need according to Your riches in glory by Christ Jesus. Your Word says that whatsoever things I desire when I pray to believe that I receive them. Therefore, I believe that my needs are supplied according to Your riches in glory by Christ Jesus.

I have given; therefore, it is given to me—good measure, pressed down, shaken together, and running over. I have abundance and there is no lack. I sow bountifully; therefore, I reap bountifully. Father, You make all grace abound toward me and I, having all sufficiency in all things, do abound to every good work. For the Lord is my Shepherd and I do not want.

The Word of God is the answer. Pray the Word—it works!

6

Importunity and Prayer

Let's look now at another passage of Scripture where Jesus is teaching His disciples to pray: *And it came to pass, that, as he was praying in a certain place, when he ceased, one of his disciples said unto him, Lord, teach us to pray, as John also taught his disciples* (Luke 11:1).

Notice that the disciple didn't say, "Teach us how to heal the sick or how to cast out demons." Neither did he ask to be taught how long to pray or when to pray, but he recognized that the power behind Jesus' ministry was the fact that *He knew how to pray accurately.*

Knowing how to pray accurately is one of the keys to victorious living.

The story is told of a missionary walking down a jungle trail in Africa, when suddenly a huge lion appeared in the trail.

Being the man of prayer that he was, the missionary fell to his knees and prayed, "Father, I pray that this will be a good Christian lion."

The lion immediately fell to the ground, put his paws together, and said, "Father, I thank You for this food. Now bless it to my body."

The missionary's prayer was answered, but he was still in trouble because it did not bring deliverance. Learn to be specific and accurate in prayer.

The disciple asked, *Lord, teach us to pray.* Jesus answered: *When ye pray, say, Our Father which art in heaven, Hallowed be thy name. Thy kingdom come. Thy will be done, as in heaven, so in earth. Give us day by day our daily bread. And forgive us our sins; for we also forgive every one that is indebted to us. And lead us not into temptation; but deliver us from evil* (vv. 2-4).

And he said unto them, Which of you shall have a friend, and shall go unto him at midnight, and say unto him, Friend, lend me three loaves; For a friend of mine in his journey is come to me, and I have nothing to set before him. And he from within shall answer and say, Trouble me not: the door is now shut, and my children are with me in bed; I cannot rise and give thee (vv. 5-7).

Notice that Jesus is asking a question here from verse 5 to verse 7. *The Amplified Bible* has the question mark at the end of verse 7, and I believe that is where it should be.

To help you understand clearly what Jesus is saying, I want to ask you the same question: Would you have a friend like that? If you went to him at midnight and said, "Company came in unexpectedly and I need a loaf of bread. Would you lend me one?" would he say, "No, you ugly thing, you ought to have come by before I went to bed. I can't give you any bread now"?

Would you *have* a friend like that? Would you want a friend like that? No, of course not. With friends like that, you wouldn't need any enemies. Now you can see what Jesus is saying. Notice He is talking about a friend. There is no relationship, no kinship here at all. He is just a friend. He wants to know if you would have a friend like that. I'm sure you have already answered it in your own mind. None of us would want a friend like that.

In the literal Greek, verse 6 reads this way: "For a friend of mine in his journey has come unto me and I have not *what I shall set before him.*" Now you can recognize this as a faith statement. He doesn't have it or see it yet, but he says, "I will set it before him."

Come Boldly To Obtain

Now the Word of God says, *Come boldly unto the throne of grace that we may obtain* (Heb. 4:16). We are to come boldly before the throne of grace— not to beg, plead, or hope that something will happen, but we should come to obtain!

This fellow came to obtain. He didn't say, "I hope you will lend me some bread." He said, "I don't have what I *shall set before him*." He didn't have it yet, but he was talking faith. It was already in his mouth.

I say unto you, Though he will not rise and give him, because he is his friend, yet because of his importunity he will rise and give him as many as he needeth (v. 8).

Now let's find out what the word *importunity* means. Much has been said about this word, and most of it has been commentary. We need to watch many of the paraphrased editions, for so much of them is the translators' and editors' own interpretation. We need to check the Greek and other references to make sure the meaning we have has not been added by man.

Some say the word *importunity* means "persistence." *To just keep on and on.* I had a fellow tell me one time: "Now that man just kept beating on the door. He just kept knocking on that door until the man came to give him bread. That is what Jesus is teaching us to do. We are to just keep asking."

That idea is not present in this passage of scripture. In fact, it is exactly opposite of what Jesus is teaching here. This is where we have missed it. This religious thinking has held people in bondage. This line of thinking has taught us that we receive from God by beating and knocking on the same door until finally we wake up God and eventually talk Him into it.

Importunity comes from two Greek words: *aneu* which means "without" and *aidos* which means "bashfulness." Therefore, a literal meaning would be "without bashfulness." It means *bare faceness or boldness (without shame)*. Because of his boldness he came even at midnight. He had faith that, even if he came at that late hour, he would receive bread. He said, "I have not *what I shall* set before him." Jesus said that man will get up and give him all that he needs.

Notice that Jesus didn't say that this actually happened. He asked us the question: "Would you have a friend like that?" We get the idea that this actually happened, but it didn't. Jesus is only using this as an illustration.

Jesus said, *Though he will not rise and give him, because he is his friend, yet because of his importunity he will rise and give him as many as he needeth.* Now hold on to the word *friend* because it is another key to understanding this scripture.

Jesus then says, *And I say unto you, Ask, and it shall be given you; seek, and ye shall find; knock, and it shall be opened unto you. For every one that asketh receiveth; and he that seeketh findeth; and to him that knocketh it shall be opened.*

The Amplified Bible reads, "Ask and keep on asking," with a footnote that says, "This is the present imperative and often repeated." It might be often repeated; but, in this instance, it is not because that would be contrary to other scriptures concerning prayer. (See Mark 11:24; John 15:7,8; 1 John 5:14,15.)

If you take that commentary to be the true meaning of this scripture, it is already distorted in your mind. Most people never read the footnote anyway, so they are left with a false impression that will defeat them in their prayer life. When you run into a situation like this, study it carefully and see if it compares to the other teachings of Jesus. Here the translators said it *could* have meant that, *but it did not* because it would refute other things Jesus taught concerning prayer.

Persistent Faith

Here are some things I want you to notice about the word *importunity. The Amplified Bible* uses the word *persistence*. The Greek means *bare faceness* or *boldness*. If you take the word *persistence* by itself, it means "to keep on, to continue, to expect or endure in the face of opposition."

Now the man came for the bread. His presence was persistent. He didn't go away but was patiently waiting to receive. It does not say that he kept on knocking. It does not say that he knocked twice. In fact, it does not say that he knocked once. He probably did, but the Bible doesn't say he did. He came to receive. He is persistent. He wouldn't leave until he had received. We also need to be that stubborn about some things.

If you say "persistence of faith," you have changed the meaning of the word *persistent*. Persistent faith does not mean faith that just keeps on asking. Persistent faith means *faith that asks once, then stands its ground until it is manifest.* **True faith asks and receives.** Persistent faith is different from persistence by itself. *It is faith that receives or takes from God.* **Faith takes.** This is what Jesus is portraying in this passage of scripture.

The Bible is an eastern book and must be interpreted as such. In the eastern countries where it was written, the people understand, "Ask once and you receive." That is consistent with Jesus' teaching on prayer. Remember He also said not to use vain repetitions and to believe that you receive when you pray.

If it does mean to ask and keep on asking, you will have to say that it also means to receive and keep on receiving every time you ask.

If a son shall ask bread of any of you that is a father, will he give him a stone? (Luke 11:11). He did not say if he kept asking, the father would finally give it to him. He is saying if your child asks for food, you would give it to him. You wouldn't make him ask a hundred more times, then change your mind. Satan would like for you to believe that is what God is like. That kind of thinking will lead you into error and hold you in bondage. Satan wants to twist the Word and distort your image of God.

Jesus said, *Ask, and it shall be given you; seek, and ye shall find; knock, and it shall be opened unto you. For every one that asketh receiveth* (vv. 9,10). Jesus said it, and you can be sure Jesus meant what He said.

Prayer Is Not Based on Friendship

There is another aspect of this parable that we need to notice. Jesus said, *Though he will not rise and give him, because he is his friend. . . .* He had a reason for saying that. He is not just throwing in unnecessary details. He is portraying a spiritual truth.

Once Jesus said to His disciples, *I call you no more servants but friends.* A friend could go to the palace of the king or some high authority, knock at the gate, and be let in immediately. If he was not a friend, they would send a servant to tell him whether or not he could come in. Jesus is no longer calling us servants, but friends.

But the Word of God does not say anything about God answering prayer on the basis of friendship. **Prayer is not answered on the basis of friendship.** It is answered on the basis of the legal contract made with God the Father. Because you have been born again, you are the seed of Abraham. Jesus Christ is the Lord of your life; you are a child of God; the Spirit of God bears witness with your spirit; you can come boldly to the throne of grace. You can say, "Father, I stand before You without fear, without condemnation, without a sense of guilt." This right or boldness is not because of friendship, but because of the new covenant.

Prayer Is Based on
Legal Documents

Because of what Jesus did, you have a legal right to come in prayer and petition God to intervene in the affairs of life and expect God to perform His part of the covenant.

God's Word is a legal document, more so than any legal document that has ever been set forth by any law of this land. Jesus is the guarantee that it will work.

The Bible is a legal contract between you, Jesus, and the Father. It is God's will *to you* and *for you*. Some people have not even read the will. They do not know what is theirs.

A contract governs at least two people: the one who made it and the one who receives it. If you had a contract, it would tell certain things you would have to do. Then it would state certain things the other party would have to do to make it valid. It is legally binding on both parties. If you don't fulfill your part, it releases the other party from performing his part. It would become void.

This is what Jesus is stating here. He wouldn't do it because he is his friend. God does not answer prayer because of friendship. He answers prayer because of a legal document, and the result is governed by the rules of this document. That document is God's Word.

Now I am not trying to get you under the Law. Don't misunderstand what I am saying. I want you to see the need of accurately stating your prayer according to the Word that Jesus taught.

He said that he wouldn't do it because he was his friend. But thank God, we have a contract with our Father and we are part of the family, joint-heirs with Jesus. This is just a friend who came to a man for bread. There is no relationship, just friendship, but we are born of God. He is our Father and we are His children.

Jesus goes on to say, *If ye then, being evil, know how to give good gifts unto your children:* **how much more** *shall your heavenly Father give. . . .*

At times we have become bogged down in this passage of scripture and have failed to see that this is not portraying God at all. He is simply showing you that prayer is not based on friendship or on need.

God answers prayer because He is your Father; you are His son and you have a covenant with Him. *He says, Ask and it shall be given you . . . For every one that asketh, receiveth.*

This runs parallel with what Jesus brought out in John 15:7, *If ye abide in me, and my words abide in you, ye shall ask what ye will and it shall be done unto you.* He didn't say, "Ask what you will, then beg, plead, and keep on asking." He said, "Ask what ye will and it SHALL BE done."

What things soever ye desire, when ye pray, believe that ye receive them and ye shall have them. You release faith when you pray. Too many times we have waited to release our faith when we see it is getting better. You know that wouldn't require any faith at all. You would know it then. Sense knowledge would tell you then. That is not faith. Release your faith when you pray.

Satan does not care how much you pray as long as it doesn't work. But when we learn that the Word of God was given to us to put us over in life and to cause us to be victorious over the evil one, we will walk in victory here on earth.

. . . they which receive abundance of grace and of the gift of righteousness shall reign in life by one, Jesus Christ (Rom. 5:17).

The Amplified Bible says, "Those who receive God's overflowing grace and the free gift of right-eousness *reign as kings in life."*

7

Confession Brings Possession

God told Israel He had given them the land, but they were to go in and possess it. The land belonged to them, yet they didn't possess it for forty years because they believed more in circumstances than in God's Word.

So we see that they could not enter in because of unbelief (Heb. 3:19). The word *unbelief* here literally means "disobedience." God said to possess it, but they said, "We are not able." So they did not obey God and they did not possess the land until all who doubted God had died.

Out of the twelve spies, Joshua and Caleb were the only two who went in to possess the land. These two held fast to their confession: "We are well able to take the land." For forty years, they held fast to that one confession and they got what they said.

Let us therefore hold fast to our confession of faith that we may possess those things that God says are ours. The promised land is not a type of heaven, as some believe, but a type of victorious living on the earth. We are well able to enter in through faith.

Mix Faith With Your Words

Israel became afraid of the giants. Fear came because of the evil report. *Fear is belief in the devil.* When you are afraid something will happen, that means you believe it will happen. If you are afraid something bad will happen, that means you have more faith in the devil's ability to hinder you than you have in God's ability to put you over.

Let us therefore fear. We can insert the word *believe* here. *Let us therefore* believe, *lest, a promise being left us of entering into his rest, any of you should seem to come short of it. For unto us was the gospel preached, as well as unto them: but the word preached did not profit them, not being mixed with faith in them that heard it* (Heb. 4:1,2).

The Word preached did not profit them because it was not mixed with faith. They didn't mix faith with what they heard.

When we pray, we must mix faith with our words. Just saying words is not prayer. *Mix faith with your words.* Israel did not mix faith with what they heard. They mixed fear with it. The mixer was the tongue. (See Num. 13:32,33.)

In Mark 11:24 Jesus tells us to believe that we receive our desires when we pray. One translation says, "Believe that you *received* them." If I do that when I pray, I must mix faith with my words: *Father, I thank You for You have heard me and I believe that I have received.*

Someone says, "Why don't you just believe it and not say anything?" Here are five reasons:

1. *He shall have whatsoever he saith* (Mark 11:23).

2. *Out of the abundance of the heart the mouth speaketh* (Matt. 12:34).

3. *We also believe, and therefore speak* (2 Cor. 4:13).

4. *So then faith cometh by hearing, and hearing by the word of God* (Rom. 10:17).

5. *For as the body without the spirit is dead, so faith without works is dead also* (James 2:26). Your words are the spirit of your faith.

Faith Cometh

So then faith cometh by hearing and hearing by the word of God (Rom. 10:17). It doesn't say it comes by reading or by having heard, but it says faith comes by *hearing* (present tense). It comes by *hearing the Word of God*. The Greek says, "Faith cometh by report and the report by the declaration of God." So faith cometh by hearing the *rhema* (spoken word) *of God*.

When we hear ourselves speaking, saying what God said, it will produce faith in us more quickly than if we hear someone else saying it. **Hearing your own voice speak God's Word will excite your heart to action.** For example, you don't always obey what someone else says, but you do obey your words. They govern you.

The Word says that the gospel did not profit them because it was not mixed with faith. They were hearers only of the Word, not doers. They didn't do what God told them. There are many people today who say, "Yes, I believe in prayer," but they are not obedient to what God has said to do when you pray.

Hold Fast Your Confession

Seeing then that we have a great high priest, that is passed into the heavens, Jesus the Son of

God, let us hold fast our profession, or our confession (Heb. 4:14).

Here is where so many have missed it. Most people hold fast to the problem. They hold fast to the sickness. We are to hold fast to our confession of faith. Our confession should agree with the Word of God. If it doesn't, it is a confession of unbelief because it agrees with the devil.

The confession of your mouth, even after you have prayed correctly, will determine whether or not you receive. If you have prayed and asked God for something, and then say, "I just don't know what I am going to do; it's just not working out," you blew it! You cancelled your prayer. That prayer will not work for you. Hold fast to the confession of your faith.

Wherefore, holy brethren, partakers of the heavenly calling, consider the Apostle and High Priest of our profession, Christ Jesus (Heb. 3:1). Actually, in Greek the word for *profession* means "confession." So we are to consider Jesus Christ, the Word, as the High Priest of the confession of our faith.

I don't know what that means to you, but here is what it means to me: When I pray speaking faith-filled words concerning the things I desire, I can see Jesus, seated at the right hand of God the Father, nudging the Father and saying, "He is holding fast to the Word, saying the same things You said; He is returning Your Word to You. Now let's perform it just the way he said it." Jesus confesses to the Father what I say *if* it agrees with the Word of God.

But if I say, "Lord, I have prayed and it is not working out," He cannot say, "Father, he has prayed, but it is not working out." The Father would say, "Those are not My words—who said that? Doesn't he know that I said he could have whatever he says, even in prayer?"

Let the Problem Go

Your confession is so vital to prayer. Your confession after prayer will either bind you to your problem or release you from it. The problem is yours and God will let you have it back if you want it. **You are the one to determine the outcome and proclaim it.**

Keys of the Kingdom

I will give unto thee the keys of the kingdom of heaven: and whatsoever thou shalt bind on earth shall be bound in heaven: and whatsoever thou shalt loose on earth shall be loosed in heaven (Matt. 16:19).

The authority of binding and loosing is on earth. You have that authority. One translation says, "You have authority to bind what is bound in heaven and to loose what is loosed in heaven."

Ask yourself, *What is bound in heaven?* The curse is bound in heaven. There is no poverty there, no sickness, no sorrow, no pain.

Jesus said we have authority to bind those things here on earth. Prayer is one of the ways to bind and loose. *Pray ye . . . Thy will be done in earth, as it is in heaven* (Matt. 6:10). How is it in heaven? What is loosed there? Abundance, life, happiness, health, joy, peace, and Jesus gave you authority to loose those things here on earth.

Words bind and loose. Your words are your bond. Your words are your authority in the earth.

. . . whosoever shall say . . . and shall not doubt in his heart, but shall believe that those things which he saith shall come to pass; he shall have whatsoever he saith. **The things you say are the things you will eventually believe. The things you believe are the things you will eventually receive.**

What will you say—poverty *or wealth?*

What will you bind—sickness *or health?*

What will you loose—fear *or faith?*

You can release the ability of God through the words of your mouth—or you can talk your problem, pray your problem, hold fast to your problem, and your problem will become greater. If you talk your problem until your neighbors start believing it, they will tell someone else about it. Soon you will have a whole group of people believing that you have a problem. Then you *do* have a problem! For Jesus said. . . . *if two of you shall agree on earth* (Matt. 18:19).

Do you see what speaking your problem will do? Don't ever talk your problem before people that believe in problems. Find someone who believes in answers from the Word, someone who will agree that the problem is removed. **Let go of the problem and cast the whole of your care over on the Lord.** (1 Peter 5:7.) **Take hold of the answer.** Hold fast to the answer until that is all you can see.

The story is told of a lady who looked out her back door and saw her three children playing with three little skunks.

She shouted, "Run, kids, run!" And they did. Each one grabbed their little skunk and took off running!

That reminds me so much of Christians who bring their problems to the altar and say, "Here is this problem, Lord," but when they get up, they take their stinky problem with them! They go home and worry about it all night. If they are worrying over it, they still have it. They haven't left it with God.

For example, let's suppose you have a watch that does not run. You take it to a jeweler and ask him to fix it for you. As you are holding it in your hand, you keep asking him when he is going to fix it. He replies, "When you give it to me." If you have the watch (problem), He can't fix it. But when He has the problem, you don't have it anymore. It is foolish to worry over something you don't have.

When you are holding on to the problem, God's hands are tied. When you turn it loose, then God can do something about it.

Casting all your care upon him; for he careth for you (1 Peter 5:7). He did not say to pray that God will take your cares. God will not take them from you. He instructs you to get rid of them by casting all your cares upon Him. He will not *take* them, but He will *receive* them.

We are to hold fast to the confession and not to the problem. Hold fast to the confession, *I believe that I receive when I pray.*

When someone says, "Things sure don't look too good," just reply, "I am not moved by how things look, or how I feel. I am moved by what I believe, and I believe that it was settled when I prayed." Jesus said, *When ye pray, believe that ye receive them and ye shall have them* (Mark 11:24).

He that believeth . . . hath (John 6:47).

He shall have whatsoever he saith (Mark 11:23).

Out of the abundance of the heart the mouth speaketh (Matt. 12:34).

A good man out of the good treasure of the heart bringeth forth good things (Matt. 12:35).

The Tongue and Health

James said that you put bits in a horse's mouth to turn its whole body and you put a rudder on a ship to turn the whole ship; so is the tongue so situated among our members that it defiles the whole body. (James 3:3,4.) If you control the tongue, the body will respond to your words. If you talk sickness, it becomes impossible to live in health. The more you believe it, the less you believe in healing. The thing you continually talk about will consume you.

Faith will only come by hearing the Word of God, and it will come more quickly when you hear yourself quoting and speaking God's Word after Him.

Why Confession Works

The Greek word in the Bible translated *confess* means "to say or speak the same thing."

The Spirit of God spoke this into my spirit just as plainly as if I heard it with my ears. I had heard some teaching concerning this on one occasion, but I didn't grasp it then. As the Spirit began to fill in the gaps for me, I could see it.

He said: *The Word says the angels are ministering spirits. These ministering spirits stand beside you daily and listen to the words that you speak. They are created beings, designed of God to minister for you, but you are the one who tells them what to do.*

The angels are ministering spirits sent to minister for you and they listen to the words you speak. You do not pray to angels, but they listen to the words you speak. They cause or allow to come to pass the things that you say. But you furnish the words of the assignment.

He directed me to Hebrews 1:14, *Are they not all ministering spirits, sent forth to minister for them who shall be heirs of salvation?*

The Holy Spirit said, *God's Word is His will for man. Man is created in the image of God, and since God created man in His own image, then man's word should be his will toward God.*

Then for the first time I really understood why it was so necessary for us to speak what we desire. **We are giving orders.**

If God's Word is His will, your word should be your will. You should never speak words that are not your will. They are not your words.

Your will and your word are one.

Don't let satan speak through you.

Wouldn't it be silly if God said one thing and willed something else? Or if He willed one thing, then said something else? That would cause confusion. You wouldn't know what was true. **God says what He wills.**

The Holy Spirit said, *Man's words should be his will toward God. The angels were designed as created beings to minister for you and they know that. They listen to the words that you speak. Every word that you speak the angels hear, for they are always beside you, waiting to hear what you choose to bind or loose. Then they are busy to perform or cause to come to pass the things you speak if they are in agreement with the Word of God. By authority of your words, they will maneuver you into a position where these things will come to pass.*

But if you speak sickness and disease, if you speak contrary to the Word of God, they will not perform it or cause it to come to pass. They will back off, fold their hands, and bow their heads, for you have bound them by the words of your mouth. Your words will either bind them or loose them. If your words bind the angels, you have bound God's messengers, and, in so doing, you have bound God.

Jesus said, I will give you the keys of the kingdom of heaven: and whatever you shall bind on earth shall be bound in heaven: and whatever you shall loose on earth shall be loosed in heaven. All heaven will stand behind your right to be healed.

Now that will jerk the kinks out of your conversation! You can *loose sickness* in your own body by *inaccurate prayer,* or you can *loose healing* by *accurate prayer.* Release God's ability by praying His words.

Let's take a look at Revelation 22:8-9:

And I John saw these things, and heard them. And when I had heard and seen, I fell down to worship before the feet of the angel which shewed me these things. Then saith he unto me, See thou do it not: for I am thy fellowservant, and of thy brethren the prophets, **and of them which keep the sayings of this book:** *worship God.*

The angel is a servant to those who keep the sayings of this book. He listens to what you say. The angel said, "Worship God! Don't worship me! I'm just doing God's bidding."

The word used in Hebrews 1:14 for *ministering spirits* really means *angelic apostles.* The ministering spirits are angelic apostles, sent to minister for us who are heirs of salvation.

Now let's look at Psalm 103:19. This verse of scripture will open your eyes of understanding in a greater measure to the things we have been talking about:

The Lord hath prepared his throne in the heavens; and his kingdom ruleth over all.

There is definitely a dual meaning here and I know this meaning is included. God's throne is in heaven, but *his kingdom ruleth over all.* Where is His kingdom? The kingdom is in us and it rules over all. The words you speak into your heart will rule.

The earth was spawned from the spirit world. It was created to be the likeness of the spiritual world which spawned it. Man was created by God to be in the likeness of God: to have dominion, to control, and to rule. *His kingdom ruleth over all,* and He set up His kingdom inside us. You feed good seed into the kingdom and it will produce the things desired.

In the beginning was the Word, and the Word was with God, and the Word was God (John 1:1). Today your word is god over your circumstances. Your word is the beginning of things. The words that you continually say will be god over the circumstances you face in life. Eventually, they will come to pass.

Notice Psalm 103:20, *Bless the Lord, ye his angels, that excel in strength, that do his commandments, hearkening unto the voice of his word.* The angels do His commandments. We are to let no corrupt communication proceed out of our mouths.

That is what He commanded us to do, but what are the angels to do? They do those things that are in line with God's Word. That is what God has assigned them to do. They are ministering spirits sent forth to minister for us in this earth.

God's Word says that man *shall have whatso-ever he saith,* if he believes and doubts not in his heart. *Whatsoever things ye desire when ye pray, believe ye receive them.* It seems then as though the angels have something to do with those prayers being answered. Now, you don't pray to angels, but they listen to what you say. They are ministering for you. Their job is to see that it comes to pass. They will work day and night in your behalf if you speak God's Word. He said they excel in strength and do His commandments, *hearkening unto the voice of His Word.*

What is the voice of God's Word? The Bible is His Word, but how do we give voice to it? By speaking His words. Then when I speak His Word, my words become the voice of God's Word.

Let's say you want wisdom. The Word says, *If any man lack wisdom, let him ask of God who giveth to all men liberally and upbraideth not, and it shall be given.* So if I put God's Word into voice, then the angels hearken unto my words. They will go about to cause the words that God spoke in my behalf to come to pass.

Let the redeemed of the Lord say so, whom he hath redeemed from the hand of the enemy (Ps. 107:2). Give voice to the Word by saying:

The spirit of truth abides in me and teaches me all things and guides me into all truths. Therefore, I confess I have perfect knowledge of every situation and every circumstance of life. The wisdom of God is formed within me. I trust in the Lord with all of my heart, and I lean not unto my own understanding. I let the Word of Christ dwell in me richly in all wisdom. I do follow the Good Shepherd; I know His voice and the voice of a stranger I will not follow.

So my angels are loosed and begin to work to cause the confusion to stop and see that I have the wisdom of God. They find ways to get it to me so I will not be deceived by the evil one. They make sure that I hear the voice of the Good Shepherd.

Faith-filled words release God and bring Him on the scene in your behalf.

There was a lady who stood up in church and said, "Pray for me. I am taking the flu." There was no need to pray; she was taking it. She didn't even wait for satan to give it to her! Nobody prayed for her, but I imagine most people said, "Oh, poor thing, she is taking the flu." So she had about fifty people believing she was taking the flu. Jesus said that if two of you agree, it will be done. Do you see the spiritual law that is set in motion by words? This earth is under God's word system.

Be careful about talking your problems because most people will agree with you.

Learn to speak the answer to the problem.

Find the answer, then feed it to the problem.

Learn to use God's system.

Unscriptural Talk Cancels Prayer

Many pray for good health and strength, but if they sneeze once, they say, "I believe I am taking the flu," or "I must be taking a cold." They have set a scriptural law in motion and it cancelled their prayer.

Let me share a little secret with you that will stop 50% of your colds if you will do it consistently. Every time you sneeze say, "Thank God, I'm taking healing. I have a choice; so I am taking healing."

I have set before you life and death, blessing and cursing: therefore choose life (Deut. 30:19).

No one will snicker or laugh when you say, "I'm taking the flu." They will just reply, "Oh, poor thing." But when you say, "I'm taking healing," they will often say, "What has gotten into you?" Just reply, "The Word of God!"

James says that the body can be controlled if you can control the tongue. Your body is like a child—it will do anything you let it do. It will be sick if you will let it. The spirit man on the inside is the one that should dominate the body. Christ redeemed you from the curse of poverty, sickness, and sin. (Gal. 3:13.)

Some would reason that if we were redeemed from the curse of the Law, then everyone would be healed and no one would be sick; but that is not true. We are redeemed from sin; but not everyone is saved. They could be, but they have not acted on God's Word to be delivered from sin. You can still sin if you want to. According to the Word of God in Galatians 3:13, we have no more right to allow sickness and disease in our bodies than we do sin. It all comes from satan!

Spirit-Ruled Body

The Greek word translated *physical body* means "slave." The physical body should be a slave to the human spirit. Sin caused the human spirit to lose control over the body because Adam became a spiritually dead man the day he sinned. He became body-ruled, not spirit-ruled; and he gained a sensual knowledge that caused his body to rebel against his spirit. The spirit man was dethroned that very hour; the human spirit lost its authority and ability to rule the body. Sin took control of the flesh. The body rose up and began to rule over the spirit.

We can now understand what Paul said in Romans 8:6: *For to be carnally minded is death; but to be spiritually minded is life and peace.*

To be carnally minded is to be body-ruled, and it produces spiritual death.

To be spiritually minded is to be spirit-ruled, and it produces life and peace, for God designed you that way.

For the law of the Spirit of life in Christ Jesus hath made me free from the law of sin and death (Rom. 8:2). God's law that produces spirit life in Christ made your spirit free from the spiritual death caused by sin.

For what the law could not do, in that it was weak through the flesh, God sending his own Son in the likeness of sinful flesh, and for sin, condemned sin in the flesh: That the righteousness of the law might be fulfilled in us, who walk not after the flesh, but after the Spirit (Rom. 8:3,4).

The Law was given for people who were body-ruled. Body-ruled people can't obey the laws of God because God wants one thing and their bodies want another. The flesh is weak; it is not subject to God's laws. All men from Adam to Jesus were body-ruled; their spirits were slaves to their bodies. It was as a satanic chain that enslaved all mankind.

Then Jesus came in the likeness of sinful flesh. He looked like other men, but God was His Father and He was spirit-ruled. He *broke* the satanic chain of spirit slavery and condemned sin that had enthroned itself in the human body. He destroyed that satanic stronghold and made it possible for men to walk in the spirit.

And if Christ be in you, the body is dead because of sin but the Spirit is life because of right-eousness (Rom. 8:10). When Christ comes into your spirit, the body dies; it is dethroned. You certainly don't want something that is dead ruling over you. The body is dead, but the spirit is life because you became righteous. The spirit man received the ability to rule the body once again.

The spirit man grows on the Word of God. God's Word is filled with faith and that feeds the spirit man. As satan taught the body to rule over the spirit with words, so must the spirit. *It is the spirit that quickeneth; the flesh profiteth nothing: the words that I speak unto you, they are spirit, and they are life* (John 6:63).

It takes time to train the spirit, but God's Words are spirit life. It is a process of training the human spirit to believe what you say will come to pass.

Say only the things that you believe will come to pass. Quit talking foolishness, sickness, and disease. Quit saying, "That tickles me to death." Satan has programmed death into the human vocabulary. It ought not to be so, for it will sap your faith.

Begin now to stop the enemy from using your vocabulary to hold you in bondage.

Study the life of Christ, and you will find that He refused to confess or admit death. You remember when He went to raise Lazarus from the dead, He wouldn't confess he was dead. He said, *He sleepeth.* Finally, He said to His disciples, *He is dead* (John 11:14). But the Greek says, "died." There is a great difference between a man that died and one that is dead. If you do not believe that, look at Jesus. He died; but, thank God, He is not dead!

Learn to control your vocabulary and never speak anything that you don't want to come to pass. Someone says, "I could never do that." If the Word says you can (and it does), then you can; but it will take some time to get all that old unbelief out so you can speak faith-filled words.

Training the Body

Your body is like a child; you can train it to obey your words.

You have trained that old dog at your house to do certain things, or maybe your cat or bird. James says that you can train every beast, bird, serpent, and thing in the sea. Mankind by his natural ability can train a dog, a bird, or any beast.

Once we had a parakeet that we trained to talk. We taught it by saying the same words over and over. My grandmother had one whose name was Toskininee. I could hardly say that name myself, but the bird could say it as clearly as anyone. It would say, "Toskininee is a pretty bird," and it would sound just like my grandmother. Parakeets don't really understand words, but they can be trained to talk.

Your dog doesn't understand either. It is the repeating over and over of the same name until the dog comes when you say that name. You train animals with words.

Now what makes you think that your body is less intelligent than a dog? What makes you think that you can't train the human body to obey the voice of your spirit by the words of your mouth? It can be done, for the body was designed to be obedient to words.

You had to train your body to pray. It had to be obedient to the spirit man. The words we speak in prayer do have a definite effect on our bodies. When we pray or continue to say the problem, the body reacts in line with our speaking or praying. *Learn to use the Word of God to control your body.*

Paul said, "Mortify the deeds of the body." How do you do that? You can't take a knife to mortify the deeds of the body; you will hurt yourself. But you can use words to put to death its deeds by training the body to react to God's Word. You can cause your body to come into subjection to your spirit.

Paul said, "I *keep* my body and bring it under lest while I preach the gospel I become a castaway." In the literal Greek, Paul actually said, "I buffet my body." *Buffet* means "to slap with an open hand or clenched fist." Train your spirit man to believe what you say will come to pass by practicing tongue control.

In the area of sickness, I believe we give place to the devil when we say, "Wonder what is wrong with me?"

The devil can then get out his little flip chart and say, "Well, would you believe you are taking the flu?"

We say, "Well, I haven't been feeling too good." Then we begin to reason, "It could be the flu. My neighbor had it last week and I went over and prayed for him. That must be where I caught it." Satan suggested it and you reasoned yourself into it!

Then your first desire is to tell someone that you believe you have the flu. If you will just quit thinking and talking about how you feel and *say what God said* (Matt. 8:17), you can stop 50% of it right there. Now don't misunderstand what I said. I didn't say that it was all in your mind. I don't deny that the disease exists—**I deny its right to exist in my body.**

Don't give place to the devil. Just refuse to give him any place. Many times the symptoms will go away if you don't embrace them. *Your body obeys your words—positive or negative, good or bad.*

Some would say, "What if I make a faith confession and still get sick?" Just keep *saying what God said.* Don't base your faith on experience, but on *God's Word.* You keep confessing

God's Word until it becomes a revelation in your spirit. It takes time to train your spirit. You may get sick several times while you are in training, but don't quit just because you are not perfected yet. It is not a fad; it is a way of life.

If you continue to say, "I am sick," your words will stop your body's resistance to that disease or virus.

A few years ago, the Lord was dealing with me about the power of words and the authority they have over the body. One morning while attending a meeting at the Lake of the Ozarks, I woke up with a headache. It was just pounding.

I seldom have a headache, and my first thought was, *I wonder what I am taking.*

Then I said, "Wait a minute! I refuse to have it."

I decided I would act on what the Lord had been showing me about Paul bringing his body into subjection. So I just slapped myself on the forehead with the palm of my hand and said, "Head, you stop that in the name of Jesus. You come into line with the Word of God."

Within two minutes, the headache was gone.

Now with other things, it has taken a longer period of time for the manifestation to come. Several years ago, I had ulcers. I received my healing by confessing God's Word over a period of about three months. Those symptoms tried to come back from time to time, but I learned to resist them instead of receiving them. I would slap my body with my hand and say aloud, *Stop that in the name of Jesus. Body, you come into agreement with the Word of God. I am healed by the stripes of Jesus.*

Someone said, "Why, that's silly." Well, it wasn't their body that was hurting. It was mine, and it worked! They do their dog that way. They slap him and say, "Stop that," or "Get out of the house." They think nothing of it. But if you slap your body and tell it what to do, they think you are strange. If your dog understands that language, you know that your body must be more intelligent than a dumb animal.

Learning To Use Your Words

Now some of these things may be a little off the subject of prayer, but these are some areas that God is wanting us to look into. Once as I was teaching on this subject, the following prophecy came forth:

For I have desired to reveal My wisdom, saith the Lord. Even in these days, I have spoken to men from time to time that there was coming in this hour men that will speak forth the Word accurately and learn to use My Word as I have set it forth.

It will come forth with great power, as the wisdom of God unfolds within man, as he understands the system that I have set in motion in this universe. All men come under that system; they walk and live under it. But when they learn to control that system by the spoken Word, **then** MY *power will come forth in them. They will be able not only to control their bodies, but they will control their minds by casting down imaginations. They will be able to rise to a* **new level of life.**

The world will stand in awe as they see these people come forth. They will say, "Who are these people that have come in this hour that are able to speak even as though they had the power to do what they speak, and it seems to come to pass even before our eyes? We don't understand these things." But it is My wisdom, saith the Lord, and it is hidden in My Word. I didn't hide it **from** *you. I hid it there* **for** *you, so you could find it and act upon it.*

Now turn not a deaf ear to that which I have spoken, for My Word shall rise within you with great revelation. For I am doing in this hour things that men have not understood, just as was prophesied in days of old. I said it by My prophets that you would not believe the reports of the things that I would do. Some will not believe, but the hour is coming that men shall proclaim My Word boldly over their own bodies, and it will cause sickness and disease to depart. Their words will cause the enemy to flee in terror.

The power of the Lord shall rise within men until there will be a race of people on this earth when I come that will stand against satan and see him flee from them. They will stand without sick-

ness or disease in their bodies. They will stand even before whole cities and proclaim, "In the name of Jesus I break the power of sin over this city." Then the walls of satan will crumble and the power of God shall be loosed in that city.

The wisdom of God shall flow unhindered and My power shall rule in the midst. Even as the darkness grows darker, the light shall grow lighter. My wisdom shall be released in greater measure and greater revelation as men take My Word at face value, even as I have spoken it.

The tongue cannot be controlled by natural ability. It is an unruly evil in the unregenerate state. But the wisdom of God that has come by the rebirth of the human spirit, imparted by the Holy Spirit to the hearts of men, will cause the tongue to come into subjection to the spirit of man, which is ordained of God to rule. It shall cause the body to conform to the Word of the living God.

The power of the Highest shall be manifest in the spoken Word. Then men shall speak My Word boldly and believe what they say will come to pass.

It will be even as though I said it. For when you mix faith with your words, it is as though I said it, for you breathe spirit life into the words that you speak. Your words shall flow forth, even as the words of Jesus when He spoke, for He said, "The words that I speak unto you, they are spirit, they are life. The flesh profiteth nothing, but the words that I speak, they are spirit and they are life."

These words have come before, but men turned a deaf ear to them. But these are the days that I am raising up a new generation of people. In My Word I have said that you do not put new wine in old bottles lest it break the bottles. You put new wine in new bottles that they will both be preserved.

When the human spirit is reborn, the Spirit of God releases creative ability within, and it becomes the new bottle that will preserve the new wine, The rebirth shall come to the front in this generation, and ye shall observe the mighty works of God in it. I have chosen a people, and I shall bring them to a land and they shall dominate it. They shall have dominion.

For I am coming for a Church that is without spot or wrinkle. I am coming for a Church that is not weak. I am coming for a Church that is victorious. I am coming, and ye shall see the manifestation of My power, for I have chosen the Church to reveal the wisdom of God to the generations and to the principalities and powers.

When men shall conform to the Word of the living God, then the power of the Highest shall flow unhindered out of their voices. Out of their mouths shall flow spirit words that will control the forces that have controlled them in days past. They will proclaim, "The enemy is defeated," and he shall be defeated. For I say that the battle is the Lord's and victory is yours. Learn to walk in victory, saith the Lord.

Thank God for sharing this so others could hear it. I had been hearing it in my spirit for months. The world is in for an eye-opener in these last days. We are tapping a source of power that is not capable of being defeated.

Here is what the Spirit of God has been saying to me for some time: *There is coming a day when the people of God will even take authority over the pestilence that we know in this hour. The world will say, "Who are these that the pestilence never touches?"*

Some of this has already happened. I know of a family who, when they built a patio on the back of the house, said, "The mosquitoes and flies are not going to keep us from using it." They took the Word of God and marched around the backyard, quoting what the Word said about being redeemed from the pestilence. People who have been there say you can be in the backyard or on that patio and you will never be bitten by a mosquito, nor will a fly bother you. But you better not try the *front* porch! That may sound silly to some, but you can't argue with success!

Practice Faith

Learn to use your words accurately, whether in prayer or in speech. Now you don't learn to operate in this overnight, just as you don't learn to drive a car or fly an airplane overnight. It is a process of learning, then putting into practice what you have learned. Learn from the Word of God; then put it into practice. **Practice your faith.**

The Word says that whatever you do will prosper (Ps. 1:3) and that no weapon formed against you shall prosper (Isa. 54:17). Learn to use these scriptures to destroy defeat. The Word says that man has dominion over the fish of the sea and the fowl of the air. When I began to see this, I started using my confession of the Word to catch more fish.

When I first learned about confession, I didn't want to get in over my head, so I said, "I'll just start using it in the little things." I would advise you to do the same. Start believing God for your next parking place when you go downtown.

Release Your Faith in Words

Even though God desires to answer the prayers and meet the needs of every individual, someone has to request it in this earth either by saying it or praying it. He already knows the problem or the need before you ask, but it seems as though God cannot move until someone on earth has requested it. He has given the authority of this earth to mankind, and He cannot violate His Word. *The heaven, even the heavens, are the Lord's: but the earth hath he given to the children of men* (Ps. 115:16).

This passage of scripture agrees with Jesus' words in Matthew 16:19, *Whatsoever thou shalt bind on earth shall be bound in heaven,* and also in Mark 11:24, *What things soever ye desire, when ye pray, believe that ye receive them, and ye shall have them.*

God cannot violate His Word. It seems as though He does not come in the earth to destroy the works of the devil unless someone on the earth uses their authority by requesting or demanding it in the name of Jesus. **The authority of the earth has been given to man.**

In Galatians 3:13 you can see that you are redeemed from the curse of the Law, which includes poverty, sickness, and spiritual death. Here again, enforce it. You must demand it in Jesus' name. You have legal authority in this earth through that name.

In Mark 16:17-18 Jesus said, *These signs shall follow them that believe; In my name shall they cast out devils; they shall speak with new tongues; They shall take up serpents; and if they drink any deadly thing, it shall not hurt them; they shall lay hands on the sick, and they shall recover.*

Jesus has given us the power of attorney to use His name, and that name is above every name. (Phil. 2:9,10.)

Ability — Authority

Prayer is one of the means of releasing the ability of God.

God has power to do anything. He has the ability to destroy the devil, but He can't do it now because of His Word. His Word is out and He will not go against it. We know what the end is going to be because the overall picture is in the Bible. Read the back of the book—**we win!** The devil will be put in the pit for a thousand years, then loosed for a little time, and finally cast into the lake of fire. But until that time, God has done all *He* is going to do about the devil. It is *your* responsibility to take care of him. *You* have dominion. *You* are to cast him out.

God's Word gives us instructions on how to use our authority to defeat satan:

Submit yourselves therefore to God. Resist the devil, and he will flee from you (James 4:7).

Be sober, be vigilant; because your adversary the devil as a roaring lion, walketh about, seeking whom he may devour; whom **resist steadfast in the faith** (1 Peter 5:8,9).

When satan comes against you, use the name of Jesus, use the authority Jesus gave you. God is not going to do it for you. The power of binding and loosing is not in heaven; it is on earth—and it is *yours.* Jesus gave believers authority to preach the gospel, heal the sick, cast out demons, and raise the dead.

The angels can't preach the gospel. In the tenth chapter of Acts when Cornelius prayed, God sent an angel to talk to him. In essence, this is what the angel said to him: "I can't preach the gospel to you, but I can tell you where there is a man who can preach the gospel. He is staying with Simon the tanner by the seashore. Go call for Peter. He will come preach the gospel to you and tell you what to do."

Have you ever wondered why the angel didn't preach the gospel to him? Because, in this dispensation, they do not have that authority.

The authority in this earth has been delivered to believers. We have the authority, but we have been praying for God to do the things He has told us to do, such as heal the sick, cleanse the leper, cast out demons, and raise the dead. (Matt. 10:1-8.) These things are as mountains before us, but God's ability can perform them. Learn to release God's ability.

Get Your Praying and Saying Together

For verily I say unto you, That whosoever shall say unto this mountain, Be thou removed, and be thou cast into the sea, and shall not doubt in his heart, but shall believe that those things which he saith shall come to pass; he shall have whatsoever he saith (Mark 11:23). Notice He said, *Those things which he saith.* He didn't say he would have what he *hoped for* or what he *prayed.* He said, "He will have what he *says.*" Evidently, *your saying can nullify your praying.*

If you pray one thing and say another, you are going to have what you *say,* not what you *pray.* But when you get your *saying* and your *praying* together, you have the spiritual forces working for you. Jesus said, "Therefore it will work in prayer." This faith principle, a principle of spiritual law, works in prayer; but we have used it in reverse.

We have prayed, "Lord, the mountain is getting bigger. I can't get over it. Move the mountain, Lord. It is getting bigger!"

God says, "But, son, I said you can have what you say."

"Yes, but, Lord, I have this problem."

"But, son, you can have what you say, even in prayer."

"Yes, Lord, but You don't understand. It is getting worse."

We have been operating it in reverse and it has caused the mountain to grow. Jesus said you are to **speak to the mountain,** not **pray to God about the mountain.** He said, *Whosoever shall say unto this mountain, Be thou removed, and be thou cast into the sea and shall not doubt in his heart, but shall believe those things which he saith shall come to pass; he shall have whatsoever he* **prayeth?** No, he will have *whatsoever he* **saith.** If you don't get your *saying* in line with your *praying,* you will be wasting your time.

God is not in the business of doing many of the things we pray for Him to do. We try to do what God is supposed to do and ask Him to do what we are supposed to do.

We say, "Lord, take all my cares." But He is not going to do that. He said we are to cast all of our cares on Him because He cares for us. (1 Peter 5:7.)

We have been doing all the caring and worrying. We pray for Him to take it from us, but He can't do that. If you cast them upon Him, He will do the caring.

Be careful for nothing; but in every thing by prayer and supplication with thanksgiving let your requests be made known unto God.

And the peace of God, which passeth all understanding, shall keep your hearts and minds through Christ Jesus.

Finally, brethren, whatsoever things are true, whatsoever things are honest, whatsoever things are just, whatsoever things are pure, whatsoever things are lovely, whatsoever things are of good report; if there be any virtue, and if there be any praise, think on these things (Phil. 4:6-8).

We have been wanting God to give us peace while we think on all the bad things. He can't do that. It is against His Word.

Just as a jeweler can't fix your watch until he has it in his possession, neither can God work out your problem until you give it to Him, or cast it over onto Him, and leave it there. Once you have prayed, don't take it up again. Just thank Him for the answer.

I remember as I was complaining about a problem with my car, a certain shop manager said to me, "I can't fix it while you are driving it down the highway at sixty miles an hour." So many people want to keep trying to work out their problems by their own rules. *They have a zeal of God, but not according to knowledge* (Rom. 10:2).

8

The Widow and The Judge

One night after I had taught on prayer, a lady said to me, "What about the woman who went to the unjust judge? She just kept going back and pestering him until finally he gave in. Isn't that what Jesus wants us to do?"

In Mark 4:24, Jesus said, *Take heed what ye hear.* When you hear something explained a certain way and you accept it, then each time you read it, hear it, or think about it, you will receive it the same way.

The Spirit of God spoke to me and said, "Study the Word of God like you have never heard it before." In other words, "Turn off your religious head when you study the Bible."

Sometimes you must turn it off to receive the truth. For instance, when you first look at the parable of the unjust judge, which that lady was referring to, it is easy to think that the widow just kept pestering the judge until he gave in to her request. Some translations indicate this, but we must realize that some areas of this translation are the result of men trying to logically reason out a meaning. It is their opinion, so they included it. If this parable means what it seems to say on the surface, then Jesus was speaking contrary to what He taught in Matthew 6:7: *when ye pray, use not vain repetitions, as the heathen do.*

An Attitude of Prayer

Let's look at this passage of scripture, so often misinterpreted and misleading to many in their praying:

And he spake a parable unto them to this end, that men ought always to pray, and not to faint (Luke 18:1). *The Amplified Bible* says, ". . . and not turn coward." **We ought always to pray.** Obviously, He doesn't mean for us to crawl around on our knees, praying all the time; but you can be in **an attitude of prayer** continually.

Here is what the Spirit of God revealed to me as I meditated and considered this scripture prayerfully: "If you have a need this morning and you prayed over it, believing that you received when you prayed, then tomorrow when some other need arises, don't faint and give up because the first prayer has not been manifested. Men ought always to pray and not faint, or turn coward and give up. They ought to pray about each need as it arises."

In Luke 18:2 Jesus begins the parable: *There was in a city a judge, which feared not God, neither regarded man:*

And there was a widow in that city; and she came unto him, saying, Avenge me of mine adversary.

And he would not for a while: but afterward he said within himself, Though I fear not God, nor regard man;

Yet because this widow troubleth me, I will avenge her, lest by her continual coming she weary me.

And the Lord said, Hear what the unjust judge saith.

And shall not God avenge his own elect, which cry day and night unto him, though he bear long with them?

I tell you that he will avenge them speedily. Nevertheless when the Son of man cometh, shall he find faith on the earth? (Luke 18:2-8)

You would not take away from that scripture, nor would you really add to it, if you said, "Will He find *that* kind of faith on the earth when He comes?"

The widow was an insignificant person. She had no authority or political power. She had no support and no one to take care of her. She was at the mercy of the people.

Listen to what Jesus said: *And there was a widow in that city; and she came unto him* (the unjust judge), *saying, Avenge me of mine adversary.* From this, some have inferred that the widow just kept coming. The only indication for this interpretation is that it says, *she came unto him,* **saying.**

You can interpret it two ways, but I choose to believe that the widow came to the unjust judge with fire in her eyes and authority in her voice; that while she was walking toward him, she was saying, *Avenge me of mine adversary.*

The literal Greek says, "She *was coming* to him *saying.*" To me, this indicates she was *coming* and *saying* at the same time. She was talking as she was walking. The literal Greek says of Jesus that on one occasion "He was coming to them saying." It doesn't really mean that He kept coming and saying the same thing. He was speaking to them as He was walking toward them.

Of the judge, Jesus said, *And he would not for a while: but afterward he said within himself. . . .* Notice this didn't happen outwardly. It happened on the inside of him. . . . *Though I fear not God, nor regard man; Yet because this widow troubleth me, I will avenge her, lest by her continual coming she weary me.* The words she spoke troubled him. Her words were filled with the authority of faith.

Notice what she said: *Avenge me of mine adversary.* She didn't waste words. She didn't say "maybe so" or "please" or "if it wouldn't be too much trouble." She demanded it. There was something about the words this widow spoke that troubled the unjust judge. It was the faith in the woman's voice that troubled him, and her request was granted.

Suppose this little widow had said to the unjust judge, "Those folks are giving me lots of trouble; let me tell you all the mean things they have done," and then had gone back home. What do you think would have happened? The unjust judge would have said, "I wonder why that woman came up here and told me all that." No, she went to him with **the answer.** She did not mention **the problem.**

146

Faith Words Dominate

There is authority in faith-filled words. The authority in the widow's words changed the unjust man's decision. Though he would not do it for a while, her words—the authority in those words—troubled him, and he finally gave in.

Many have thought Jesus was teaching us to keep pestering God until we finally wear Him down. This could never be representative of God. This was an *unjust judge,* who had all the qualities of satan. The authority in the widow's voice changed the decision of the unjust judge. **Her words changed his mind.**

Jesus said, *The words that I speak unto you, they are spirit, and they are life* (John 6:63). The words that Jesus spoke are not just printed pages. They are spirit life. When you get them on the inside of you, they will transform your spirit. They will cause you to speak words of faith, driving out defeat and bringing victory.

Jesus said, *Hear what the unjust judge saith.* People try to relate the unjust judge to God, but how can you compare an unjust judge to God? If we do that, we have missed the whole point of what Jesus was teaching. Let's rightly divide the Word of Truth:

Though I fear not God, nor regard man; Yet because this widow troubleth me, I will avenge her, lest by her continual coming she weary me. In other words, "That woman meant what she said. I know by the tone of her voice, she will be back."

The unjust judge is only troubled. He is not weary yet. But her continual coming would cause him to be weary. Since he is not weary yet, evidently she has not been coming. She only came once. He said, I will *avenge her,* **lest** *by her continual coming she weary me.* The unjust judge granted her request so she wouldn't come back.

God Will Avenge Speedily

The Lord said, *Shall not God avenge his own elect, which cry day and night unto him, though he bear long with them?* He is not saying they were crying day and night over the same thing; yet we have read that into it. We have had the same idea here as in the first verse when Jesus said, *Men ought always to pray, and not to faint.*

In other words, "If you have a need this morning, pray about it. If it is not manifest and you have another need tonight, don't sit around wringing your hands, saying, 'Since God didn't answer my first prayer, He'll not answer this one.'"

God has to bear long with us at times. But that is because we are not in line with the Word of God and we try to do it our way.

There have been times when I have prayed about everything and just thrown out a scatter load, hoping to God some of it would work. Once in a while, some of it would and I would be surprised. That is what you call a "faith accident." You finally come across something that you believe, and it happens.

Jesus said, *I tell you that he* (God) *will avenge them speedily.* The unjust judge did not avenge speedily, but Jesus said that God would avenge us speedily. *Nevertheless when the Son of man cometh, shall he find faith on the earth?* Will He find the kind of faith this woman possessed? Even though she was so insignificant in the eyes of the public, she went to the unjust judge—a man who feared neither God nor man—and her request was granted.

Will the Son of man find that kind of faith when He comes back?

The Unjust Judge

There was in a city a judge, which feared not God, neither regarded man. As we have noted, he would qualify for the devil. It certainly could not be God.

The unjust judge is representative of the evil one, or satan. The widow represents the individual believer. Jesus is showing us the power of speaking boldly. Within ourselves, we are insignificant. Without Christ, we can do nothing; but, praise God, we are not without Him!

Jesus said, *Hear what the unjust judge saith.* Now when Jesus says hear something, He means to pay special attention to it. Hear what satan will say when a believer comes to him and demands boldly, "Avenge me of my adversary." As believers today we would say, "I demand my rights in Jesus' name."

This little woman was coming in the authority of her faith. She was representative of believers who dare to walk by faith and not by sight. The unjust judge is representative of satan who is subject to the authority of faith-filled words. When the Son of man returns, will He find this kind of faith on the earth—that a believer would dare to stand before the unjust one and tell him what to do?

This not only portrays the individual believer using his authority, but also the Church using the name of Jesus. Isaiah 54:4-5 says she *shalt not remember the reproach of thy widowhood any more. For thy Maker is thine husband; the Lord of hosts is his name.*

Ephesians 3:9-10 outlines the role the Church is to play: *And to make all men see what is the fellowship of the mystery, which from the beginning of the world hath been hid in God, who created all things by Jesus Christ: To the intent that now unto the principalities and powers in heavenly places might be made known by the church the manifold wisdom of God.*

What principalities and powers is he talking about? The same principalities and powers mentioned in Ephesians 6:12, *For we wrestle not against flesh and blood, but against principalities, against powers, against the rulers of the darkness of this world, against spiritual wickedness in high places. He is saying, For we wrestle . . . against principalities, against powers, against the rulers of the darkness of this world, against spiritual wickedness in high places.* He is talking about the devil, his angels, and all his evil forces.

*To the intent that now unto the principalities and powers might be known **by the church** the manifold wisdom of God.* The Church is going to reveal the manifold wisdom of God, showing that God was in Christ reconciling the world to Himself, declaring His righteousness for the remission of sins that are past and bestowing on us His righteousness. The Church can come forth wearing the breastplate of righteousness and the helmet of salvation, having our loins girt with the Truth and our feet shod with the gospel of peace, with the shield of faith in our hands and the Sword of the Spirit in our mouths.

We can come boldly before the unjust judge and say, "In the name of Jesus, get your hand off me, off of my finances, off of God's property! I am redeemed from the curse and delivered from the powers of darkness!"

Dominion

In the first chapter of Genesis, God told Adam to dominate this earth—take dominion over it and subdue it. This was not only for the earth, but also for all that was in it. In other words, if anything got out of line, Adam was to put it back in line. This was Adam's responsibility, but he didn't do what God commanded. He turned his authority over to the evil one. He bowed his knee to an outlaw spirit.

The Church today stands in a position that is parallel to that of Adam in the beginning. We can either bow our knee to the outlaw spirit and give in to the things that the enemy puts before us, or we can stand boldly against him with the name of Jesus and break his ability to deceive. We have authority to demand deliverance from our adversaries through the name of Jesus.

The Righteousness of God

You may be just as I was when I first heard of the believer's authority. I thought, *Man, I wouldn't dare do that. I might make the devil mad.*

The real reason I wouldn't do it was because I had no revelation in my spirit of who I was in Christ. I was like the desperately ill man whose charismatic friend suggested he rebuke the devil and command him to leave. He replied, "Look, I am not in any position to antagonize anyone!"

Thank God, I found out satan is no match for the believer who knows his authority and position in Jesus Christ! When you are born again, you become the righteousness of God and a joint-heir with Jesus. All that Jesus has is yours. His righteousness is imputed to you. *For He hath made him to be sin or us, who knew no sin; that we might be made the righteousness of God in him* (2 Cor. 5:21). *He hath raised us up together, and made us sit together in heavenly places in Christ Jesus* (Eph. 2:6).

When you stand before satan, he doesn't see you—he sees the authority of Jesus. The Word says you are the righteousness of God, created in Christ Jesus unto good works which God ordained. (Eph. 2:10.) We have sung those old unbelieving songs so long that we thought it was true. "Just a weary pilgrim, struggling through this world, I know not today what tomorrow will bring, shadows, sunshine or rain."

Paul said, *For thy sake we are killed all the day long; we are accounted as sheep for the slaughter.* Most people stop right there, but the next verse says: **nay,** *in all these things we are more than conquerors through him that loved us* (Rom.

8:36,37). He quoted the first scripture out of context to magnify his positive statement. No, we are not as sheep led to the slaughter. That is talking about Jesus and His crucifixion. We are **more than conquerors** through Him that loved us. We are conquerors through Jesus. One who is more than a conqueror is one who enjoys the victory, but doesn't have to fight the battle. Jesus won it for us. Thank God, everything He did, He did for us!

Sometimes when you talk like this, people will say, "Who does he think he is?"

I think I am who the Word says I am: *the right-eousness of God, a joint-heir with Jesus, a world-overcomer, more than a conqueror!*

Someone else might say, "But the Word says, 'There is none righteous, no not one.'" That is true. There is none righteous within himself. But, thank God, I am not in myself. I am in Christ. Man's righteousness is as filthy rags in the sight of God. I am not declaring my own righteousness. I am declaring His righteousness. (Rom. 3:25,26.) I do not see myself in this position of authority

because of my own righteousness but because of
His. Paul said, *Awake to righteousness, and sin
not* (1 Cor. 15:34).

Redeemed That the Blessings Might Come

One of the problems with many religious
people is that they try to do good things to merit
favor with God. We are living under grace, not the
Law. If you try to do good works to build up credit
with God, the Word says you put yourself under the
curse of the Law. *For as many as are of the works
of the law are under the curse* (Gal. 3:10). To be
under the curse of the Law means to be subject to
the curses, which are poverty, sickness, and spiritual death.

Christ redeemed us from the curse of the Law
that the blessing of Abraham might come on the
Gentiles through Jesus Christ. (Gal. 3:13-15.) I am
a child of God and an heir with Jesus. Abraham's
blessings are mine: The Word says he was blessed
coming in and blessed going out, blessed in the city

and blessed in the field. He was blessed all over more than anywhere else!

We need to realize that when we were redeemed from the curse of the Law, we were NOT redeemed from the blessings. They belong to us. If you have been born again, Abraham's blessings are yours. **We are the redeemed**—not going to be someday, we are now! *Let the redeemed of the Lord say so, whom he hath redeemed from the hand of the enemy* (Ps. 107:2).

Some might ask, "Why do we still get sick if we are redeemed from the curse of the Law?"

Let me ask you another question: Jesus redeemed the world from sin, didn't He? Then why do folks still sin? They are redeemed from sin, yet they go on sinning. You see, you can do it if you want to. Just because we are redeemed from the curse of the Law doesn't mean that no one will ever sin or be sick again. Redemption is yours, but you must walk in it.

Paul said, "Sin shall not have dominion over you." It shouldn't have, but it is up to you. You must mortify the deeds of your flesh. Just as the children of Israel had to go in and possess the land that God had given to them, we must use our authority to command sickness and sin to stay out of our lives. We have been redeemed from the curse of the Law, but we must go in and possess that which is already ours. Redemption is our land.

If ye be willing and obedient, ye shall eat the good of the land (Isa. 1:19).

9

Prayer Armor

Before we end this book, we must look at one more passage of scripture concerning prayer that sums up much of what has been said: Ephesians 6:10-18. Here Paul is talking about prayer armor:

Finally, my brethren, be strong in the Lord, and in the power of his might. Put on the whole armour of God, that ye may be able to stand against the wiles of the devil (vv. 10,11). Notice Paul did not say, "Be strong in your own might," but "in the Lord." It is His might. It is not something we have to work up to. We must simply be obedient and be clothed in His might.

Put on the whole armor or, as the Greek says, the *complete* armor of God.

Would you know the armor of God if you saw it? It is God's clothes and He is clothed in righteousness. He gave you His clothes to wear. Our problem has been that when we get ready to pray, we take off our breastplate of righteousness and throw it in the corner, saying, "Lord, I am so unworthy. I am so no good."

I can just imagine how God feels about such statements. He probably says, "Can you believe what they are saying! I sent My Son. He suffered and died to make them righteous. I gave them My clothes to wear, but they are laying over in the corner. Then they tell Me how unworthy they are because they don't have anything to wear." That must grieve the heart of God after all He has done to clothe us with righteousness. Be obedient and put on His armor. You need it!

For we wrestle not against flesh and blood, but against principalities, against powers, against the rulers of the darkness of this world, against spiritual wickedness in high places.

Wherefore take unto you the whole armour of God, that ye may be able to withstand in the evil day, and having done all, to stand.

Stand therefore, having your loins girt about with truth, and having on the breastplate of righteousness;

And your feet shod with the preparation of the gospel of peace;

Above all, taking the shield of faith, wherewith ye shall be able to quench all the fiery darts of the wicked (vv. 12-16).

Did you ever notice it says, "**All** the fiery darts of the wicked"?

Someone may say, "Yes, but I just can't do it." I beg your pardon! The Word says you can.

"Yes, but you see, I am so unworthy."

Now you have told on yourself. You do not have on the whole armor of God. You left off the breastplate of righteousness.

"Yes, but I don't feel righteous, so I must not be."

You may not feel like getting dressed in the morning before you go to work, but believe me, it is the thing to do! God has told us to put on all of His clothes. If you don't feel righteous, it is because you don't have on your breastplate.

The Church has been too sin-conscious. We need to become righteous-conscious. There is not a Christian who doesn't know about sin, but how many know that they are the righteousness of God? Renew your mind to the fact that you are the righteousness of God in Christ. When it becomes a revelation in your spirit, sin will cease to be a problem for you. It will be as Paul said, "Sin shall not have dominion over you."

The Sword of the Spirit

Above all, taking the shield of faith, wherewith ye shall be able to quench all the fiery darts of the wicked. And take the helmet of salvation, and the sword of the Spirit, which is the word of

God (vv. 16,17). **The Sword of the Spirit.** The spoken Word of God is the Sword of the Spirit.

We call the Bible our sword, but it is not really the sword. It may be the substance the sword is made of, but it is not the sword until it proceeds out of your mouth. There is no life in the Bible until it comes out of your mouth. You can lay the Bible on someone that is sick and it will not heal them. There is no power in the book. The power is released when you believe it and speak it.

You breathe life into it and the Spirit of God rises up in you when you dare to say, "Father, Your Word says that my need would be supplied according to Your riches in glory. I have given, and now it is given to me good measure, pressed down, shaken together, and running over. In the name of Jesus, I receive it."

In the Greek, there was little or no punctuation. The translators just simply punctuated as they believed it should be. I believe from studying verses 17 and 18 that Paul is saying, "the sword of the Spirit, which is the word of God praying always."

The Word of God Praying

When you pray the Word of God, you are praying the perfect will of God. It will tear down satan's stronghold.

Hebrews 4:12 says, *For the word of God is quick, and powerful, and sharper than any twoedged sword, piercing even to the dividing asunder of soul and spirit, and of the joints and marrow, and is a discerner of the thoughts and intents of the heart.*

The Word of God is alive and powerful, more powerful than any tongue that could speak against you. That is the twoedged sword he is talking about. One translation says, "The Word of God is a living thing." Revelation 1:16 says, *And out of his* (Jesus') *mouth went a sharp twoedged sword.*

The tongue will cut or heal. *There is that speaketh like the piercings of a sword but the tongue of the wise is health* (Prov. 12:18). The Word of God is health to all our flesh. (Prov. 4:22.) Therefore we should proclaim it.

You might pray this way: *I am redeemed from the curse of the Law; and in the name of Jesus, I refuse to bow to sickness or disease. Every disease germ and every virus that touches this body dies instantly, in the name of Jesus.*

Then make that your confession every day, not just when you feel like it. Your body is like a child. It will do anything you let it do, and sometimes it would rather be sick than have to go to work.

For the flesh lusteth against the Spirit, and the Spirit against the flesh: and these are contrary the one to the other: so that ye cannot do the things that ye would (Gal. 5:17). If you give in to the flesh continually, your body will be sick. Galatians 5:19-21 lists the works of the flesh. Each one, or any combination of these, is very capable of producing sickness and disease in the body. Paul said, If *ye live after the flesh, ye shall die: but if ye through the Spirit do mortify the deeds of the body, ye shall live* (Rom. 8:13).

No, this is not the power of positive thinking. It is the power of God's Word. It is creative power—

the ability of God released when you pray the Word of God.

Take the things God has said about your situation and put them in prayer form. Here is a simple way to pray the Word of God:

Father, in the name of Jesus, I am the body of Christ. I overcome evil with good. Satan has no power over me for the Greater One dwells in me. Greater is He that is in me than he that is in the world. No evil will befall me; neither shall any plague come nigh my dwelling, for He has given His angels charge over me. They keep me in all my ways and in my pathway is life.

I thank You, Father, that no weapon formed against me will prosper, but whatever I do will prosper. I am like a tree planted by the rivers of water.

My God supplies all my needs according to His riches in glory by Christ Jesus. I have all sufficiency in all things. I do abound to all good works for my God has made all grace abound toward me.

Every word is based on the Word of God. You are proclaiming the answer, not the problem.

Someone says, "You don't understand. I don't have abundance." No, and you never will if you continue to disagree with God. Learn to call those things that be not as though they were. It is when you continually agree with and proclaim boldly the things God has said about you that He will perform His Word. Most Christians have tried it for a day or two, then given up. For nearly two years I prayed the Word of God before some things became a revelation in my spirit.

Just because we have said it two or three times doesn't mean we believe it. Sometimes it is necessary to say it over and over to bring faith. The Bible says, *Faith cometh by hearing, and hearing by the word of God.* If we hear ourselves speaking what God said, it will get in our spirits more quickly than if we hear someone else say it. **If we confess God's Word audibly, faith will come more quickly.**

The Helmet of Salvation

And take the helmet of salvation, and the sword of the Spirit, which is the word of God: praying always with all prayer and supplication in the Spirit, and watching thereunto with all perseverance and supplication for all saints (vv. 17,18). **Praying always with all prayer. The Word of God praying.** Paul is talking about prayer armor.

Part of that armor is the helmet of salvation. The word *salvation* means "deliverance, preservation, healing, and soundness." All those ideas are present in the word *salvation* and they all belong to us. David said, *Let the redeemed of the Lord say so, whom he hath redeemed from the hand of the enemy* (Ps. 107:2). Many people are not walking in the full provision of salvation because they are not saying it. They remain in the hand of the enemy. (2 Tim. 2:24-26.)

Deliverance, healing, preservation, and soundness belong to us. Jesus paid for it! (Isa. 53:4,5.)

170

The Breastplate of Righteousness

Come before the Father in prayer, wearing the breastplate of righteousness. Then you can stand in the throne room and say, "Father, I stand before You because of the righteousness of Your Son Jesus. I come boldly before You without fear or condemnation or a sense of inferiority."

Someone may say, "You mean you think you are not inferior to God?" I didn't say I wasn't. It is *His* righteousness that is not inferior. I am a partaker of that righteousness. (2 Cor. 5:21.) The Word says I am a joint-heir with Jesus. Do you think Jesus is inferior?

We are the righteousness of God in Christ Jesus. God's righteousness cannot be inferior or unworthy.

When you put all this armor on, you will have on God's clothes. When you stand before the devil to resist him, he thinks God is inside that armor, and He really is. (John 14:23.) With God's armor on, satan doesn't see you; he sees God's clothes. But the minute you raise up your helmet and say, "I prayed, but it isn't working out," or "I don't feel healed," satan knows that it is not God because He doesn't talk that way.

Put on the prayer armor. Gird your loins with the Truth, for this part holds all the armor in place. If you do not have the Truth, you are defeat going somewhere to happen! If you do not have the Truth, you do not know how to pray accurately. If you do not have the Truth, you will not know who you are in Christ Jesus.

Prayer is your legal right to come to God's throne, wearing the breastplate of righteousness and the helmet of salvation with your loins girt about with the Truth, your feet shod with the gospel of peace, holding up the shield of faith, and having the Sword of the Spirit in your mouth.

The heart of the wise teacheth his mouth (Prov. 16:23).

Charles Capps a farmer from England, Arkansas became an internationally known Bible teacher by sharing practical truths from the Word of God. His simplistic, down to earth style of applying spiritual principles to daily life has appealed to people from every Christian denomination.

The requests for speaking engagements became so great after the printing of *God's Creative Power® Will Work for You* that he retired from farming and became a full-time Bible teacher. His books are available in multiple languages throughout the world.

Besides publishing 24 books, including best-sellers *The Tongue A Creative Force* and *God's Creative Power®* series which has sold over 6 million copies, Capps Ministries has a national daily radio broadcast and weekly TV broadcast called "Concepts of Faith".

For a complete list of CDs, DVDs, and books
by Capps Ministries, write:

Capps Ministries
P.O. Box 69, England, Arkansas 72046

Toll Free Order Line (24 hours)
1-877-396-9400

E-Books & MP3's Available

www.cappsministries.com
Visit us online for:

Radio Broadcasts in Your Area
Concepts of Faith Television Broadcast listings:
Local Stations, **Daystar**, & **TCT** Television Network

youtube.com/CappsMinistries
facebook.com/CharlesCappsMinistries

BOOKS BY CHARLES CAPPS AND ANNETTE CAPPS

Angels

God's Creative Power® for Finances

God's Creative Power® - Gift Edition
(Also available in Spanish)

BOOKS BY ANNETTE CAPPS

Quantum Faith®

*Reverse The Curse in
Your Body and Emotions*

Removing the Roadblocks to Health and Healing

Overcoming Persecution

BOOKS BY CHARLES CAPPS

NEW RELEASE! - Calling Things That Are Not

Triumph Over The Enemy

When Jesus Prays Through You

The Tongue – A Creative Force

Releasing the Ability of God Through Prayer

End Time Events

Your Spiritual Authority

Changing the Seen and Shaping The Unseen

Faith That Will Not Change

Faith and Confession

God's Creative Power® Will Work For You
(Also available in Spanish)

God's Creative Power® For Healing
(Also available in Spanish)

Success Motivation Through the Word

God's Image of You

Seedtime and Harvest
(Also available in Spanish)

The Thermostat of Hope
(Also available in Spanish under the title
Hope- A Partner to Faith)

How You Can Avoid Tragedy

Kicking Over Sacred Cows

The Substance of Things

The Light of Life in the Spirit of Man

Faith That Will Work For You

Powerful Teaching From Charles Capps

If you have enjoyed reading this book, you can find more dynamic teaching from Charles Capps in these revolutionary books.

Can Your Faith Fail?

Faith That Will Not Change

Have you ever stepped out in faith only to later feel that you have failed? If you are like most Christians, at some point in your life, you have questioned the word God gave you.

The truth, however, is that faith is a law and God's laws always work. This is a practical guide to encourage you in your walk with God. It will teach you how to put your faith into action to produce results in your life.

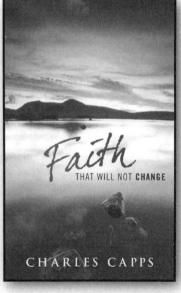

ISBN-13: 978-0-9819574-6-3

Understanding Paul's "Thorn In The Flesh" And How You Can Overcome The Messenger Of Satan Assigned To You

Triumph Over The Enemy

In Second Corinthians 12:7, Paul writes about "a thorn in the flesh, the messenger of Satan" who had been sent to harass him. This "messenger" was sent to create problems and stir up the people against Paul everywhere he preached. But Paul knew the key to overcoming this obstacle – he learned to exercise his God-given authority here on the earth!

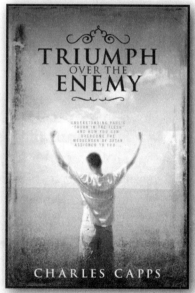

This book will show you how to walk in God's grace and triumph over this enemy sent to harass and keep you from God's greater blessings in your life.

ISBN-13: 978-0-9819574-2-5

NEW RELEASE!!!

Removing the Roadblocks to Health and Healing

In order to receive healing and live in health, you must prayerfully evaluate your life as a whole and allow the Holy Spirit to guide you into wellness.

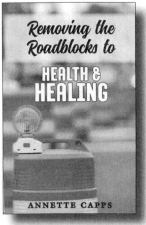

In this book, Annette Capps gives a insightful, practical look at the emotional and spiritual hindrances that believers face daily.

Recognizing and removing these roadblocks can enable you to receive healing and walk in health and wholeness.

- Claiming Sickness as Belonging to You
- Belief in Tribal DNA
- Using Infirmity as a Tool
- Holding on to Negative Emotions
- Refusing to Forgive
- Feeding the Spirit of Infirmity
- Ignoring the Leadings of the Holy Spirit and Your Spirit
- Staying in an Unhealthy Environment
- Trying to Act Beyond Your Faith
- Believing You Will Be Healed in the Future

ISBN 13: 978-1-937578-58-9

Seedtime and Harvest

God's Word is incorruptible seed, and God's promises are seeds for harvest. In this book you will learn that as you speak God's promises out of your mouth as a seed, it goes into your heart to grow and produce a harvest of blessing.

ISBN-13: 978-0-9819574-3-2

The Thermostat of HOPE

Surely no one would be foolish enough in natural things to argue with you when you turn the thermostat to 70 degrees, but they will when you set your goal on God's promises.

Hope, like a thermostat, is simply a goal-setter with no substance. Faith, which comes from the heart, is the substance of what you desire.

The heart (spirit) of man is like the heart of the heating-cooling unit. Designed by God to produce the very thing you plant in it. You plant it or set the goal by speaking it!

ISBN-13: 978-1-937578-30-5

YOUR SELF-IMAGE DETERMINES THE DIRECTION OF YOUR LIFE.

The business world discovered years ago that a person will never rise above the image they have of of themselves. Success or failure is reflected by that image.

What or who you imagine yourself to be determines your fate in life. Your self-image can carry you to heights of success or plunge you into the depths of defeat and despair.

GOD CREATED YOU IN HIS OWN IMAGE

God sees you as created in His image and likeness, endued with the power and authority of Jesus' name and the ability to succeed. That is the image He wants us to have of ourselves.

When we become a new creation in Christ, we can be transformed by renewing our minds to what God's Word declares us to be.

God doesn't see you the way you once were. If you are born again, the Bible says you are the righteousness of God in Christ. Change the image you have of yourself and it will change the direction of your life!

ISBN-13: 978-0-9618975-9-8

Words Are The Most Powerful Force In The Universe

The Tongue A Creative Force - Gift Edition

The words you speak can cause you to experience freedom and increase, or cause you to live a life of bondage and lack. Most people do not realize the power of their tongue. It is the ultimate creative force, and this dynamic potential is inside of you.

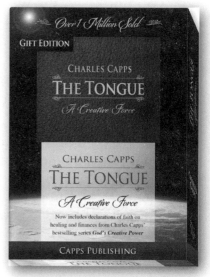

God's Word that is conceived in your heart, then formed by the tongue, and spoken out of your own mouth, becomes a spiritual force releasing the ability of God within you.

ISBN-13: 978-0-9819574-8-7

Speak Life and Live Better, Stronger and Longer!

Join the millions whose lives have been changed by the *God's Creative Power*® Series. This dynamic series from Charles Capps has sold over 5 million copies. Each book reveals powerful teaching on the power of your words and includes scriptural confessions that will change the way you think and the way you live.

God's Creative Power® *Will Work for You—*
Over 4 Million Sold!

Charles Capps' original mini-book reveals that the power of the spoken word can change your destiny. God created the universe by speaking it into existence. He has given the same ability to you through your words. To be effective in life, you must speak words of faith. Let faith-filled words put you over! (Also available in Spanish)

ISBN-13:978-0-9820320-6-0

God's Creative Power® *for Healing—*
Over 1.5 Million Sold!

This powerful book combines all new teaching with Scripture confessions for healing. You will learn how you can release the ability of God for your healing with the words of your mouth. (Also available in Spanish)

ISBN-13:978-0-9820320-0-8

God's Creative Power® for Finances—
By Charles Capps
and Annette Capps

Words are the most powerful things in the universe today. They can make the difference in your finances and your well-being. Learn to turn your financial situation around by following the powerful principles of faith contained in this book.

ISBN-13: 978-0-9820320-1-5

God's Creative Power® Gift Collection—
By Charles Capps
and Annette Capps

This Gift Collection is now available and includes all three books in beautiful Italian faux leather. A perfect gift for any occasion for you and your loved ones!

(Also available in Spanish)

ISBN-13:978-0-9820320-3-9

New Release!!!

Calling Things That Are Not

The Powerful Realm of the Unseen

The principle of calling things that are not as though they were is the spiritual principle through which everything physical becomes manifest. God created light by calling for "light" when only darkness was there. Jesus used this same method, call the lepers clean, and the dead to life, and peace to the storm.

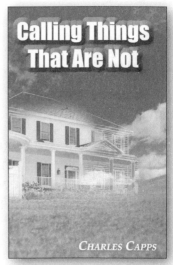

You must call for what you desire. If you want your dog to come, you call the dog. You call for what is not there. Whatever you call in the natural will come. Call what does not exist and continue to call until it manifests.

ISBN 13: 978-1-937578-31-2